Introduction to Sanskrit

Part One

Thomas Egenes, Ph.D.

POINT LOMA PUBLICATIONS, INC.

ISBN: 0 - 913004 - 69 - 3

First Printing: 1989
Second Printing: 1990

POINT LOMA PUBLICATIONS, INC.
P.O. Box 6507
San Diego, California 92106

TABLE OF CONTENTS

INTRODUCTION

REASONS FOR STUDYING SANSKRIT

There are several reasons to study the subtle and refined language of Sanskrit. The sound, script, grammar, and systematic nature of the language is charming in itself, something of great beauty. The study of Sanskrit creates orderliness within the mind because Sanskrit is a highly systematic language, reflecting the orderliness of nature itself.

Most students who study Sanskrit also have an interest in the content of the Sanskrit literature. This large body of literature is enormously diverse, including such fields as philosophy, science, art, music, phonology, grammar, mathematics, architecture, history, education, and logic (to name just a few). The literature can be understood in greater depth when it is studied in its original language.

Even a little Sanskrit will give you control over English translations of the Sanskrit literature, so you will be able to decide if a crucial word has been mistranslated. While you may not become an expert translator of the Sanskrit literature, you'll find that an introductory knowledge of Sanskrit has great worth. Even a small knowledge of Sanskrit is useful when reading Sanskrit texts in English. And who knows? The study of Sanskrit could lead to something far beyond what you anticipated.

VEDIC AND CLASSICAL SANSKRIT

Sanskrit (**saṃskṛta**) means "perfected," or "put together" ("put," **kṛta** and "together," **saṃ**). Sanskrit is divided into two principal parts: Vedic Sanskrit and Classical Sanskrit. The older language is Vedic Sanskrit, or Vedic, the language of the **Saṃhitā** and

Brāhmaṇa, the two principal parts of the Ved. Vedic Sanskrit begins with the ***Ṛg-Ved***. Classical Sanskrit, which includes several aspects, is the language of the ***Bhagavad-Gītā***, ***Rāmāyaṇa***, and the rest of the Sanskrit literature.

This text focuses on the beginning study of Classical Sanskrit. Normally, Vedic Sanskrit is studied after Classical Sanskrit is learned.

FEATURES OF THIS TEXT

Some of the features of this text are:

- Small, learnable steps
- Sequential organization
- A balance between alphabet, grammar, and vocabulary in each lesson
- As few unnecessary complications as possible
- Gradual integration of **sandhi** rules

Introductory textbooks or grammars for Sanskrit have been written by only a few Western scholars, including: Antoine, Coulson, Goldman and Sutherland, Gonda, Hart, Lanman, MacDonell, Perry, Tyberg, Whitney, and Wilson. This text is written to fulfill a need that still remains, which is to make the introductory study of Sanskrit simple, concise, and systematic, thereby making it more accessible and enjoyable for a beginning student. The text is not a complete survey of Sanskrit grammar, or even a primer. It is meant to be more of a "pre-primer," a basic step-by-step introduction to the fundamental aspects of the language.

After completing this text, you should be able to study any of the above Sanskrit textbooks more comfortably, or begin Part II of this text. Part II will feature the reading of selected verses from the ***Bhagavad-Gītā***, accompanied by a more thorough explanation of unfamiliar rules of grammar as they are encountered in the reading. Both volumes together will cover the basic rules of Sanskrit grammar. For college classes, Part I covers the standard material for a one-semester course and Part II for the second semester. After completing Part II, the student should be able to read the ***Bhagavad-Gītā*** with the aid of a Sanskrit dictionary and a word-by-word English translation.

In this text, each lesson has three sections:

1. Alphabet
2. Grammar
3. Vocabulary

ALPHABET

1. The study of any language begins with the study of the alphabet—both pronunciation and script. From the beginning, the pronunciation of Sanskrit should be relaxed and natural, without straining to sound "Indian." It will be helpful to imitate the pronunciation of a qualified person. As you listen to different Sanskrit recitations, you may notice that there is some slight variation in pronunciation (**ai**, **au**, **ṃ**, **ḥ**), because Sanskrit has been pronounced slightly differently in different parts of India.

   Also included in this section will be the study of the script (**devanāgarī**). The **devanāgarī** script will be studied gradually over the first seven lessons. In those lessons, the exercises will be in roman script. Beginning in the seventh lesson, the exercises will be given in both roman and **devanāgarī** script. Once **devanāgarī** has been thoroughly learned, the exercises will be in **devanāgarī** only.

One great challenge for the beginning student is learning the rules, called **sandhi** rules, which describe how the sounds of words change in different environments. In the past, students have found these rules demanding, because they cannot be used until they are memorized, and they are difficult to memorize without being used.

By introducing **sandhi** in small steps that are easy to master, this text attempts to overcome this problem. Beginning in Lesson 2, the exercises will be given without **sandhi** (**pada-pāṭha**), but will also be observed with **sandhi** (**saṃhitā-pāṭha**). Beginning in Lesson 8, the **sandhi** rules will be given in chart form, so that the charts can be used temporarily as a quick reference to gain understanding of the general context of the rules. One of the charts (given in Lesson 9 for final **s**) is structured to be conceptual, allowing the student to assimilate an understanding while using the chart. After using the charts for some time, it will be easy to memorize the rules, which begin in Lesson 13.

GRAMMAR

2. The study of grammar is from **Vyākaraṇa**, of which the primary text is the ***Aṣṭādhyāyī*** of **Pāṇini**. The ***Aṣṭādhyāyī*** is a concise and complete grammar of Sanskrit, containing about 4,000 **sūtras**, or aphorisms. While **saṃskṛta** means to "put together," **Vyākaraṇa** means to "undo" or to "take apart." It gives the details of the structure of the language.

Many of the grammatical terms are given in Sanskrit. Memorizing these terms will be useful for several reasons. It will give you a better understanding of the tradition from which these rules came. It will allow you to feel more comfortable when studying more advanced Sanskrit textbooks, of which many use these terms. It will increase your vocabulary, which will be useful in many areas, since most of these terms are also found in other areas than grammar.

VOCABULARY

3. According to **Yāska's *Nirukta*** (the **Vedāṅga** dealing with word meaning), all Sanskrit words can be divided into four categories: verbs (**ākhyāta**), nominals (nouns, pronouns, and adjectives) (**nāman**), prefixes (**upasarga**), and indeclinables (**nipāta**). Verbs, as well as nominals, are systematically derived from verb roots (**dhātu**), of which there are about 2,000.

In this text, the limited vocabulary is aimed at eventually providing you with an entry into the reading of the ***Bhagavad-Gītā*** and the ***Rāmāyaṇa***.

HOW TO STUDY THIS TEXT

Review the alphabet, grammar rules, and vocabulary frequently and in a relaxed state of mind before doing the exercises. Then the exercises will be more enjoyable, with fewer difficult areas. The exercises in this text contain as few idiomatic Sanskrit expressions as possible, so that you will not be overburdened with learning too much at one time. If the exercises seem difficult, you should review more. The answers to the exercises are given in the back of the text (p. 242).

In general, you should review as often as possible during the day, taking a few minutes to bring the material to mind. If there is any hesitation in recall, immediately look at the written form, rather than straining and thus "programming" your mind to forget. The best way to memorize is to speak the words out loud, if possible. Memorization should be easy, comfortable, and frequent.

ACKNOWLEDGEMENTS The following individuals have kindly offered inspiration and creative suggestions, and have cheerfully assisted in the preparation of this text: Bryan Aubrey, Michael Davis, Lawrence Eyre, Peter Freund, Shepley Hansen, Park Hensley, Alicia Isen, Lee Keng, John Kremer, John Konhaus, Margaret Lerom, Dawn Macheca, Devorah McKay, Meha Mehta, Christine Mosse, Dafna O'Neill, David Reigle, Beatrice Reilly, Beth Reilly, John Roberts, Robert Roney, William Sands, Peter Scharf, Barney Sherman, Thomas Stanley, Carol Stansberry, Jan Storms, Agnes Maria Von Agris, Douglas Walker, Monica Weinless, Geoffrey Wells, and Julan White. Of the more than 500 students who have studied with this text, many have given valuable and much-appreciated feedback. Dr. John Roberts, Professor of Sanskrit and Hindi at the University of Virginia, developed the **devanāgarī** typeface used in this text. My wife, Linda, assisted in editing and offered continuous guidance and support.

DEDICATION

This book is dedicated with appreciation and gratitude to His Holiness Maharishi Mahesh Yogi, who has described Sanskrit as the language of nature, the language of the impulses of the unified field of natural law. Maharishi has explained how the ancient rishis of the Himalayas cognized, in their silent meditations, impulses within pure consciousness. These cognitions were recorded in the Vedic literature, a vast body of beautiful and exhilarating expressions that describe the mechanics of evolution in every field of life. Over the years, Maharishi has emphasized the most significant passages from this literature, of which many are included in the section of this text entitled "Sanskrit Quotations." The knowlege contained in these expressions can be found at the foundation of every culture and tradition.

1

LESSON ONE

Alphabet:	The vowels in roman script The first six vowels in **devanāgarī**
Grammar:	How a verb is formed The singular ending for verbs
Vocabulary:	The verbs √**gam** and √**prach** The word for "and" How to write simple sentences

ALPHABET: VOWELS

1. In Sanskrit, each letter represents one and only one sound (**varṇa**). In English, the letter "a" may indicate many sounds, but not so in Sanskrit. The alphabet is systematically arranged according to the structure of the mouth.

2. There are two basic divisions to the alphabet:

   a. Vowels (**svara**, or sounded)
   b. Consonants (**vyañjana**, or manifesting)

3. Vowels can be either short (**hrasva**) or long (**dīrga**). Short vowels are held for one count (**mātrā**), and long vowels are held for two counts. Some vowels are called simple (**śuddha**), and some are called complex (**saṃyukta**).

	SHORT	LONG
Simple	**a**	**ā**
	i	**ī**
	u	**ū**
	ṛ	**ṝ**
	ḷ	
	LONG	LONG
Complex	**e**	**ai**
	o	**au**

4. In Vedic Sanskrit, but rarely in Classical Sanskrit, there are also vowels held for three counts, called **pluta**, which are marked in **devanāgarī** and roman script by the short vowel followed by the numeral 3. For example: **a**3, or **a** times 3. You may also see it marked with a long vowel: **ā**3. A commentary on **Pāṇini** (1.2.27) compares the three counts to the calling of a rooster: **u ū u**3.

5. Here is the pronunciation of the vowels:

a	like the first "a" in	America
ā	like the "a" in	father
i	like the "i" in	in
ī	like the "ee" in	beet
u	like the "u" in	suit
ū	like the "oo" in	pool
ṛ	like the "ri" in	river (usually not rolled)
ṝ	like the "ri" in	river (held longer)
ḷ	like the "lry" in	jewelry
e	like the "a" in	gate
ai	like the "ai" in	aisle
o	like the "o" in	pole
au	like the "ou" in	loud

6. The lines and dots are called "diacritics," or "diacritical marks." They are used because the Sanskrit alphabet has more letters than the English alphabet. Diacritics are combined with roman letters to represent new sounds.

7. A vowel by itself, or a consonant or group of consonants followed by a vowel, is called a syllable (**akṣara**).

8. Sanskrit is written in the **devanāgarī** script. The word **devanāgarī** means the "city (**nāgarī**) of immortals (**deva**)." There are no capital letters.

9. The ideal way to learn the script will be to memorize approximately one letter each day, writing it 20 times or so, and putting it on a flash card (**devanāgarī** on the front and roman on the back). Continue to practice regularly with your flash cards throughout the course. Practice for small amounts of time, several times a day.

10. Here are six vowels in **devanāgarī**. The small numbers inside each letter indicate the order in drawing the various parts of the letter. In general, write left to right, top to bottom, writing the bar last.

GRAMMAR: VERBS

1. Sanskrit roots are divided into ten classes (**gaṇa**) in order to form the present stem. We will study the four classes whose stems end in **a**. The root, written with √ before it, forms a stem (**aṅga**), and the stem adds an ending (**tiṅ**) to form a verb (**tiṅanta**).

Root	**√gam**	go
Stem	**gaccha**	go
Verb	**gacchati**	he, she, or it goes
	I______II__I Stem + Ending (**ti**)	

2. Verbs are in three persons (**puruṣa**): third (**prathama**, or first), second (**madhyama**, or middle), and first (**uttama**, or last). (Students in the West have normally learned these "upside down.")

Third person	he, she, or it
Second person	you
First person	I

3. The stem stays the same, but the ending changes for each person. This form is called the present indicative, because it is in the present tense, and it indicates. It is singular (**eka-vacana**).

Third person	**gacchati** (**gaccha + ti**)	he goes
Second person	**gacchasi** (**gaccha + si**)	you go
First person	**gacchāmi** (**gaccha + a + mi**)	I go

VOCABULARY

1. Here is the vocabulary in Sanskrit and in English. Each verb appears in its root form, followed by the third person singular form. The stem can be found by removing the endings.

SANSKRIT	ENGLISH
√**gam** (root) **gacchati** (3rd per sing)	he goes
ca (indeclinable*)	and (**ca** is placed after the last word of the series, or after each word.)
√**prach** (root) **pṛcchati** (3rd per sing)	he asks

*Some words do not have endings, and so are called "indeclinable" (**avyaya**). Included as indeclinables are: prepositions, adverbs, particles, conjunctions (like **ca**), and interjections. A few nouns are also treated as indeclinables.

2. Here are some sample sentences:

gacchāmi	I go. (or) I am going.
pṛcchati gacchāmi ca	He asks and I go.
pṛcchati ca gacchāmi ca	He asks and I go.
gacchasi ca pṛcchasi ca	You go and you ask. (or) You go and ask.

EXERCISES

1. Memorize the vowels and their order in roman script. Learn to pronounce them correctly.

2. Learn to write and recognize the first six vowels in **devanāgarī**.

3. Memorize the forms for the first, second, and third person singular verbs in the present indicative.

4. Memorize the vocabulary.

5. Translate the following sentences into English. Compare with the correct answers given in the back of the text on page 242.

   a. **pṛcchasi ca gacchati ca**
   b. **gacchāmi pṛcchāmi ca**
   c. **pṛcchati ca gacchati ca**
   d. **gacchasi pṛcchāmi ca**
   e. **pṛcchati pṛcchāmi ca**
   f. **gacchasi ca gacchati ca**
   g. **pṛcchāmi gacchasi ca**
   h. **pṛcchati ca gacchāmi ca**

6. Translate the following sentences into Sanskrit:

   a. I go and I ask.
   b. You ask and he goes.
   c. He asks and you go.
   d. He goes and asks.
   e. You ask.
   f. I ask and you go.
   g. I go and you go
   h. He goes and you go.

2

LESSON TWO

Alphabet:	Most of the consonants and how they are organized The last seven vowels in **devanāgarī**
Grammar:	Verbs in the dual
Vocabulary:	More verbs The word for "where"

ALPHABET: CONSONANTS

1. The first 25 consonants, called stops (**sparśa**), are arranged according to five points of articulation (**sthāna**):

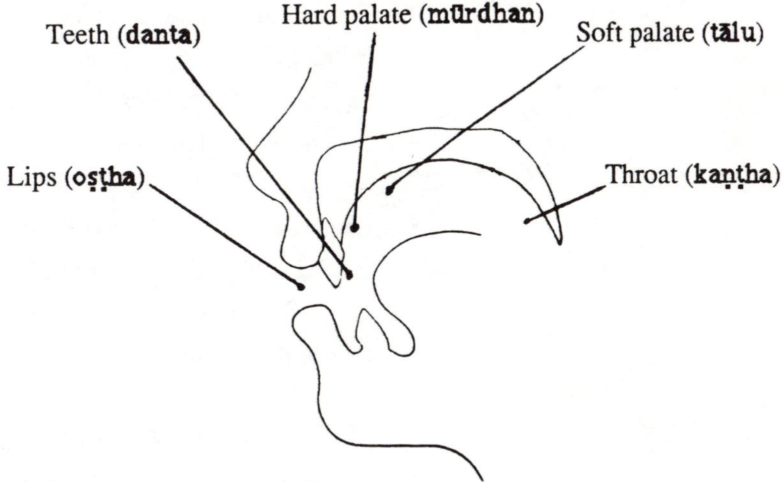

2. Here are the five sets (**varga**), arranged according to point of articulation. For example, all the consonants in the velar row (**ka varga**), are pronounced in the throat. The labial row is pronounced at the lips. The **a** is added for the sake of pronunciation.

	1st	2nd	3rd	4th	5th
Velar (**kaṇṭhya**)	**ka**	**kha**	**ga**	**gha**	**ṅa**
Palatal (**tālavya**)	**ca**	**cha**	**ja**	**jha**	**ña**
Retroflex (**mūrdhanya**)	**ṭa**	**ṭha**	**ḍa**	**ḍha**	**ṇa**
Dental (**dantya**)	**ta**	**tha**	**da**	**dha**	**na**
Labial (**oṣṭhya**)	**pa**	**pha**	**ba**	**bha**	**ma**
		Aspirated		Aspirated	Nasal
			Voiced	Voiced	Voiced

3. Each set of English letters represents one Sanskrit sound. For example, **gh** is one sound. It is the aspirated, voiced velar.

4. The sound **ka** is called **kakāra** ("ka" maker). The sound **ga** is called **gakāra** ("ga" maker), and so on. The only exception is that **ra** is not called **rakāra**, but just **ra** or **repha**, "snarl." (In the next lesson we will learn **ra**.)

5. Each row is divided into five sounds: the first (**prathama**), the second (**dvitīya**), the third (**tṛtīya**), the fourth (**caturtha**), and the fifth (**pañcama**). For example, **ka**, **ca**, **ṭa**, **ta**, and **pa** are all first in their rows.

6. Some sounds are aspirated (**mahā-prāṇa**)—more breath is used in pronouncing these sounds. Some are unaspirated (**alpa-prāṇa**). Some are voiced (**ghoṣavat**)—the vocal chords are used in pronouncing these sounds. Some are unvoiced (**aghoṣa**). The **n̄**, **ñ**, **ṇ**, **n**, and **m** are called nasals (**anunāsika**).

7. Here is how the consonants are pronounced:

k	like the "k" in	skate
kh	like the "kh" in	bunkhouse
g	like the "g" in	go
gh	like the "gh" in	loghouse
n̄	like the "n" in	sing
c	like the "c" in	cello
ch	like the "ch" in	charm (using more breath)
j	like the "j" in	just
jh	like the "j" in	just (using more breath)
ñ	like the "n" in	enjoyable

ṭ	like the "t" in	stable (for this group the tongue is touching the hard palate, as in the diagram on page 9.)
ṭh	like the "t" in	table (using more breath)
ḍ	like the "d" in	dynamic
ḍh	like the "dh" in	redhead (using more breath)
ṇ	like the "n" in	gentle

In English, we normally pronounce "t" and "d" somewhere between these two groups (retroflex and dental).

t	like the "t" in	stable (tongue at base of teeth)
th	like the "t" in	table (using breath, tongue at base of teeth)
d	like the "d" in	dynamic (tongue at base of teeth)
dh	like the "dh" in	redhead (using breath, tongue at base of teeth)
n	like the "n" in	gentle (tongue at base of teeth)

p	like the "p" in	spin
ph	like the "ph" in	shepherd
b	like the "b" in	beautiful
bh	like the "bh" in	clubhouse
m	like the "m" in	mother

7. Here are the remaining vowels in **devanāgarī**:

ṛ ऋ

ṝ ॠ

ḷ ऌ

e ए

ai ऐ

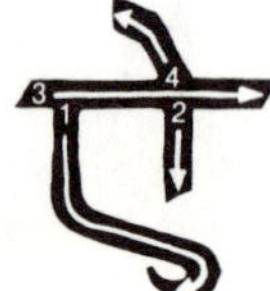

o ओ

au औ

GRAMMAR: DUAL VERBS

1. Unlike English, Sanskrit has dual verbs. The dual (**dvi-vacana**) is formed like this:

Third person	**gacchataḥ** (**gaccha + taḥ**)	those two go
Second person	**gacchathaḥ** (**gaccha + thaḥ**)	you two go
First person	**gacchāvaḥ** (**gaccha + a + vaḥ**)	we two go

(We will learn the pronunciation of **ḥ** in the next lesson.)

2. In English, interrogative words usually begin with "wh," such as where, when, etc. In Sanskrit, interrogative words usually begin with **k**. The word for "where" is **kutra**. It is usually placed at the beginning of a sentence. The other words do not need to be rearranged to make a question out of the sentence. For example:

    kutra gacchati
    Where is he going?

3. To translate **kutra gacchati** into English, first write "where" for **kutra** and then write "he goes" for **gacchati**. Literally it would then be translated as "Where he goes?" However, it is important to form correct English sentences. For "Where he goes?" you must write "Where is he going?" or "Where does he go?"

VOCABULARY

SANSKRIT	ENGLISH
kutra (indeclinable)	where
√**bhū** (root) **bhavati** (3rd per sing)	he is, he becomes (you are, I am)
√**vas** (root) **vasati** (3rd per sing)	he lives
√**smṛ** (root) **smarati** (3rd per sing)	he remembers

SANDHI

Before doing the exercises, we will have an introduction to **sandhi**, the rules for how sounds are combined. In English, we say "an apple" but "a pear." The word "the" is often pronounced differently, depending upon the following word. Some sounds change, depending upon their environment. In Sanskrit, many sounds make these same changes, and unlike English, all of these changes are written. The rules for these changes are called **sandhi**, which means "junction," "putting together," or "combination."

The exercises in Lesson 1 are written the same even after **sandhi** rules have been applied. However, in Lesson 2 the sentences would be written differently if they were to appear in a Sanskrit text. At this point, however, you do not need to learn these rules. Just observe the sentences in parentheses, and notice that these sentences are written slightly differently with **sandhi**.

EXERCISES

1. Learn the five sets of consonants, their order, and their pronunciation. Learn to write the last seven vowels in **devanāgarī**.

2. Be able to identify each consonant by its classification. For example, the aspirated, voiced palatal is **jha**.

3. Learn the dual endings for verbs.

4. Learn the vocabulary.

5. Translate these sentences, using the summary sheet on page 17. Just observe the sentences in parentheses with **sandhi**. (See page 14.)

   a. **kutra vasāvaḥ**

      (**kutra vasāvaḥ**)

   b. **bhavasi ca bhavāvaḥ ca**

      (**bhavasi ca bhavāvaś ca**)

   c. **vasāmi smarataḥ ca**

      (**vasāmi smarataś ca**)

   d. **pṛcchathaḥ ca smarati ca**

      (**pṛcchathaś ca smarati ca**)

   e. **kutra gacchāvaḥ**

      (**kutra gacchāvaḥ**)

   f. **kutra bhavāmi**

      (**kutra bhavāmi**)

   g. **kutra gacchāmi**

      (**kutra gacchāmi**)

h. **pṛcchāmi ca smarati ca**

(pṛcchāmi ca smarati ca)

i. **vasasi ca gacchāvaḥ ca**

(vasasi ca gacchāvaś ca)

j. **kutra gacchasi**

(kutra gacchasi)

6. Translate the following sentences into Sanskrit:

a. Where are you two going?

b. I live and those two live.

c. We two ask and those two remember.

d. You go and he goes.

e. Where am I going?

f. I am and you two are.

g. Where are you? (Use the singular.)

h. Where is he going?

SUMMARY SHEET

	Singular	Dual
Third	**gacchati** (he, she goes)	**gacchataḥ** (they two go)
Second	**gacchasi** (you go)	**gacchathaḥ** (you two go)
First	**gacchāmi** (I go)	**gacchāvaḥ** (we two go)

VERBS

√gam	**gacchati**	he goes, she goes
√prach	**pṛcchati**	he asks
√bhū	**bhavati**	he is
√vas	**vasati**	he lives
√smṛ	**smarati**	he remembers

INDECLINABLES

kutra	where
ca	and

3

LESSON THREE

Alphabet:	The remaining letters in roman script
	The first ten consonants in **devanāgarī**
Grammar:	The plural
	The grammatical terms to describe a verb
	Accent
Vocabulary:	More verbs

ALPHABET: THE REMAINING LETTERS

1. The previous consonants are sometimes referred to as "stops," because they stop the flow of air. They are formed by "complete contact" (**spṛṣṭa**). The remaining letters are consonants, but they allow more flow of air.

2. There are four consonants, formed by "slight contact" (**īṣat-spṛṣṭa**), called semi-vowels. They are considered to be between vowels and consonants, and so are called **antaḥstha**, or "in-between":

   ya, ra, la, va

3. The sibilants are formed by "half contact" (**ardha-spṛṣṭa**). They are called **ūṣman**, or "heated":

   śa, ṣa, sa

4. The aspirate (sometimes classified as a sibilant) is:

   ha

5. Here is how these sounds are pronounced:

y	like the "y" in	yes
r	like the "r" in	red
l	like the "l" in	law
v	like the "v" in	victory (but closer to a "w")

ś	like the "sh" in	shine
ṣ	like the "c" in	efficient (similar to the **ś**)
s	like the "s" in	sweet
h	like the "h" in	hero

6. Two additional sounds are the **anusvāra** and the **visarga**:

   ṃ (**anusvāra**)

   ḥ (**visarga**)

7. The **anusvāra** (**ṃ**) causes the last portion of the vowel before it to be nasal (like the French word "bon"). The **anusvāra** changes its sound according to its environment. It may sound like the nasal of the set to which the sound following it belongs. For example, **Śaṃkara** is pronounced like **Śaṅkara**. In the dictionary, the **anusvāra** is found in the same place as the nasal to which it refers. If the **anusvāra** comes before a semi-vowel or sibilant, it is found in the dictionary before **ka**.

8. The **visarga** (**ḥ**), or **visarjanīya**, is an unvoiced breathing that occurs in some contexts instead of an **s** or **r**. In modern India it is often pronounced as an echo of the vowel before it. After an **a** it would be a short **ha**. After an **i** it would be a short **hi**. But after **ai**, it is a short **hi**. After **au**, it is a short **hu**:

   aḥ = **ah**^{a}
   iḥ = **ih**^{i}
   uḥ = **uh**^{u}
   aiḥ = **aih**^{i}
   auḥ = **auh**^{u}

9. We have now learned all the letters in their transliterated form (their roman letter equivalents). There are other ways of representing some letters. At times you may see:

śa	as	**sha** or **ça**	(**Śaṃkara**, **Shaṃkara**, **Çaṃkara**)
ṛ	as	**ri**	(**Ṛg Veda**, **Rig Veda**)
ṃ	as	**ṁ**	(**Śaṃkara**, **Śaṁkara**)
cha	as	**chha**	(**chandas**, **chhandas**)
ca	as	**cha**	(**ṛca**, **richa**)

10. All the sounds can be classified according to the part of the mouth they come from:

Velar	**a**	**ā**			**ka**	**kha**	**ga**	**gha**	**ṅa**		**ha**
Palatal	**i**	**ī**	**e**	**ai**	**ca**	**cha**	**ja**	**jha**	**ña**	**ya**	**śa**
Retroflex	**ṛ**	**ṝ**			**ṭa**	**ṭha**	**ḍa**	**ḍha**	**ṇa**	**ra**	**ṣa**
Dental	**ḷ**				**ta**	**tha**	**da**	**dha**	**na**	**la**	**sa**
Labial	**u**	**ū**	**o**	**au**	**pa**	**pha**	**ba**	**bha**	**ma**	**va**	

The complex vowels are pronounced at two points of contact: **e** (which can be said to be composed of **a** and **i**) and **ai** (composed of **ā** and **i**) are both velar and palatal. The sounds **o** (composed of **a** and **u**) and **au** (composed of **ā** and **u**) are both velar and labial.

11. Here is the entire alphabet:

VOWELS (**svara**)

Simple (**śuddha**)	a	ā
	i	ī
	u	ū
	ṛ	ṝ
	ḷ	
Complex (**saṃyukta**)	e	ai
	o	au
Nasalization (**anusvāra**)		ṃ
Aspiration (**visarga**)		ḥ

CONSONANTS (**vyañjana**)

Velar (**kaṇṭhya**)	ka	kha	ga	gha	ṅa
Palatal (**tālavya**)	ca	cha	ja	jha	ña
Retroflex (**mūrdhanya**)	ṭa	ṭha	ḍa	ḍha	ṇa
Dental (**dantya**)	ta	tha	da	dha	na
Labial (**oṣṭhya**)	pa	pha	ba	bha	ma
Semi-vowels (**antaḥstha**)		ya	ra	la	va
Sibilants (**ūṣman**)		śa	ṣa	sa	ha

13. Here are the first ten consonants in **devanāgarī** script. Each symbol includes the sound **a**. For example, **ka** and not just **k** is meant by the first symbol.

GRAMMAR: THE PLURAL

1. Here is the plural (**bahu-vacana**) for the verb √**gam**:

Third person	**gacchanti** (**gaccha - a + anti**)	they (all) go
Second person	**gacchatha** (**gaccha + tha**)	you (all) go
First person	**gacchāmaḥ** (**gaccha + a + maḥ**)	we (all) go

2. Now we have the complete conjugation (or verbal paradigm) for the present indicative (**laṭ**):

Singular	Dual	Plural
gacchati	**gacchataḥ**	**gacchanti**
gacchasi	**gacchathaḥ**	**gacchatha**
gacchāmi	**gacchāvaḥ**	**gacchāmaḥ**
he goes	those two go	they all go
you go	you two go	you all go
I go	we both go	we all go

3. Students of Sanskrit in India memorize these paradigms horizontally. Students in Europe and America have learned them vertically. You may do either.

4. Verbs can be classified in four basic ways: tense/mood, voice, person, and number. This is similar to, but slightly different from, how verbs are classified in English. Here is a simplified overview:

Tense/Mood: The tenses and moods are grouped together in the ten **lakāra**, or "l" sounds, because they are each abbreviated by **Pāṇini** with a word beginning with **l**. We have learned the present indicative (abbreviated as **laṭ**). Other tense/moods are the perfect (**liṭ**), the periphrastic future (**luṭ**), the simple future (**lṛṭ**), the subjunctive (**leṭ**), the imperative (**loṭ**), the imperfect (**laṅ**), the optative or potential (**liṅ**), the aorist (**luṅ**), and the conditional (**lṛṅ**).

Voice: We have learned the active voice (**parasmai-pada**), which takes active endings. In Lesson 9 we will learn the middle voice (**ātmane-pada**), which takes middle endings. Usually, when the fruit of an action comes back to the agent (**ātman**), the **ātmane-pada** is used. When the fruit of an action goes to another person (**para**), the **parasmai-pada** is used (although this distinction has not been strictly followed in the literature). Some roots are conjugated in either voice and some in one voice only. Although all the verbs we have learned so far are conjugated in both voices (**ubhaya-pada**), they are seen most often in the active voice.

Person: We have learned the three persons (**puruṣa**):

Third (**prathama**)	he, she, or it
Second (**madhyama**)	you
First (**uttama**)	I

Number: We have learned the three numbers (**vacana**):

Singular (**eka**)
Dual (**dvi**)
Plural (**bahu**)

5. Each verb may be classified according to these categories. For example, **gacchati** (he goes), is present indicative, active, third person, singular.

6. Using abbreviations, called parsing codes, we could identify **gacchati** as: pres indic, act, 3rd per, sing—present indicative, active, third person, singular. (This isn't as hard as it may seem, since all verbs so far are present indicative and active. All we need to determine is the person and number.)

7. Here are some examples :

gacchāmi	I go	pres indic, act, 1st per, sing
bhavanti	they are	pres indic, act, 3rd per, pl
pṛcchāvaḥ	we both ask	pres indic, act, 1st per, dual

ACCENT

1. Accent consists of higher and lower tones (**svara**). There is a raised tone (**udātta**), an unraised tone (**anudātta**), and a "moving" tone (**svarita**). In the ***Ṛg-Ved*** the **udātta** is unmarked, the **anudātta** is marked by a low horizontal bar, and the **svarita** is marked by a high vertical bar. For example:

   ऋचो अक्षरे परमे व्योमन्

   In classical Sanskrit texts, the accents are not marked.

2. In most Sanskrit dictionaries, a mark is placed over the **udātta** for Vedic words only. For example:

   Mánu
   mádhu
   rátna

3. **Pāṇini** does not give rules for stress accent.

4. For now, an important rule for proper pronunciation is to maintain a clear distinction between the short and long vowels (discussed on page 2 and 3).

VOCABULARY: MORE VERBS

SANSKRIT	ENGLISH
na	not (placed before the verb)
√**vad** (root) **vadati** (3rd per sing)	he says, he speaks
√**sthā** (root) **tiṣṭhati** (3rd per sing)	he stands

All vocabulary is given in the order of the Sanskrit alphabet.

An additional rule you'll need to know to do these exercises is that when **ca** is used to join more than one word (such as **na gacchati**), it is put in second position. For example:

gacchāmi na ca gacchati
I go and she does not go.

EXERCISES

1. Learn the pronunciation and order of the semi-vowels, sibilants, **anusvāra**, and **visarga**. Learn the first ten consonants in **devanāgarī**.

2. Write, in correct order, the entire alphabet (in transliteration, or roman script).

3. Conjugate each verb we have learned.

4. Be able to give the parsing code for each form we have learned.

5. Translate the following sentences into English, using the summary

sheet on page 30. Underneath each sentence is the sentence with **sandhi**. Just observe the sentence with the **sandhi**.

a. **vadati na ca vadāmi**
(**vadati na ca vadāmi**)

b. **vadathaḥ smarataḥ ca**
(**vadathaḥ smarataś ca**)

c. **na gacchanti**
(**na gacchanti**)

d. **tiṣṭhāmaḥ gacchāmaḥ ca**
(**tiṣṭhāmo gacchāmaś ca**)

e. **bhavathaḥ ca vasathaḥ ca**
(**bhavathaś ca vasathaś ca**)

f. **kutra bhavasi**
(**kutra bhavasi**)

g. **tiṣṭhanti gacchanti ca**
(**tiṣṭhanti gacchanti ca**)

h. **na ca pṛcchati na ca vadati**
(**na ca pṛcchati na ca vadati**)

6. Translate these sentences into Sanskrit. Unless "two" is used, it will be understood that the plural form is intended.

a. Where are they going?

b. We do not speak.

c. He asks and they speak.

d. Where are we standing?

e. Where do those two live?

f. We are not going.

g. I ask and they remember.

h. Where are we?

SUMMARY SHEET

	Singular	Dual	Plural
Third	**gacchati** (he, she goes)	**gacchataḥ** (they two go)	**gacchanti** (they all go)
Second	**gacchasi** (you go)	**gacchathaḥ** (you two go)	**gacchatha** (you all go)
First	**gacchāmi** (I go)	**gacchāvaḥ** (we two go)	**gacchāmaḥ** (we all go)

VERBS

√gam	**gacchati**	he goes
√prach	**pṛcchati**	he asks
√bhū	**bhavati**	he is
√vad	**vadati**	he speaks, he says
√vas	**vasati**	he lives
√sthā	**tiṣṭhati**	he stands
√smṛ	**smarati**	he remembers

INDECLINABLES

kutra	where
ca	and
na	not

4

LESSON FOUR

Alphabet: Ten more consonants in **devanāgarī**

Grammar: The nominative case
The accusative case

Vocabulary: Nouns that end in short **a**

ALPHABET

1. Here are ten more consonants to learn:

ट	ठ	ड	ढ	ण
ṭa	ṭha	ḍa	ḍha	ṇa

त	थ	द	ध	न
ta	tha	da	dha	na

GRAMMAR: NOUNS

1. Sanskrit nouns (**subanta**) are formed in a similar way as verbs—there is a stem (**prātipadika**), and endings (**sup**) are added to it. Nouns are put into various cases (**vibhakti**, division), depending upon their role in the sentence.

2. We will learn two cases. The nominative (**prathamā**) is used for naming the subject, as in "Rāma goes." The nominative is also used for a predicate identified with the subject, as in "Rāma is the king." In India, words are normally cited independently in the nominative, or naming case.

   The accusative (**dvitīyā**) is the direct object. The accusative is also the object of motion, as in "He goes to the city."

3. For example, in the sentence, "The man goes to the horse," the word "man" would be in the nominative and the word "horse" would be in the accusative.

   The man goes to the horse.
   (nominative) (accusative)

4. Here is the formation of masculine nouns whose stems end in **a**:

   Stem: **nara** (masculine) man

	Singular (**eka-vacana**)	Dual (**dvi-vacana**)	Plural (**bahu-vacana**)
Nominative	**naras**	**narau**	**narās**
Accusative	**naram**	**narau**	**narān**

5. The verb and subject must agree in number in both English and Sanskrit. For example, if the subject is singular, then the verb must also be singular:

The man goes to the horse.	(Subject and verb are singular.)
The men go to the horse.	(Subject and verb are plural.)

6. The direct object need not agree with either the subject or verb. We are learning the rules for the agent construction (**kartari prayoga**), in which the agent of action (**kartṛ**) is in the nominative, and the object of action (**karman**) is in the accusative.

7. A noun in apposition, such as "Rāma, <u>the boy</u>," is put in the same case as the noun it follows. For example, in the sentence "She speaks to Rāma, the boy," both "Rāma" and "boy" are accusative.

8. The normal word order is:

subject	direct object	verb	
naras	**aśvam**	**gacchati**	(without **sandhi**)
(**naro**	**'śvaṃ**	**gacchati**)	(with **sandhi**)
the man	to the horse	goes	

Because **naras** ends in **s**, we know that it is the man who is doing the going and not the horse. While English relies on the order of the words, Sanskrit relies more on the word endings for meaning.

9. Articles, such as "the" or "a," must be put in the English translation as needed.

VOCABULARY

SANSKRIT	ENGLISH
aśva (masculine)	horse
gaja (masculine)	elephant
nara (masculine)	man
putra (masculine)	son
mṛga (masculine)	deer
rāma (masculine)	Rāma
vā (indeclinable)	or (used like **ca**)

Nouns will be cited in their stem form because that is how they appear in most dictionaries.

Nouns, as well as verbs, may be connected with **ca** and **vā**. When two nominatives are connected with **vā**, the verb agrees with the nominative closest to it, as in English. For example:

> **aśvas gajās vā gacchanti** (without **sandhi**)
> (**aśvo gajā vā gacchanti**) (with **sandhi**)
> The horse or the elephants go.

"He goes" is **gacchati**. "The man, he goes," is **naras gacchati** (with **sandhi**, **naro gacchati**). However, when there is a subject, the "he" is dropped. Then **naras gacchati** (**naro gacchati**) would be translated as "The man goes."

EXERCISES

1. Continue to learn the consonants in **devanāgarī**.

2. Memorize the singular, dual, and plural forms for the masculine nouns ending with a short **a** (like **nara**) in the nominative and accusative.

3. Learn the vocabulary and continue reviewing all vocabulary from past lessons.

4. Translate the following sentences into English, using the summary sheet. Continue to observe the **sandhi**.

   a. **narās mṛgam smaranti**
   (narā mṛgaṃ smaranti)

   b. **rāmas aśvau gacchati**
   (rāmo 'śvau gacchati)

   c. **kutra gajās vasanti**
   (kutra gajā vasanti)

   d. **narau rāmam vadataḥ**
   (narau rāmaṃ vadataḥ)

   e. **putras smarati pṛcchati vā**
   (putraḥ smarati pṛcchati vā)

   f. **rāmas mṛgam gacchati**
   (rāmo mṛgaṃ gacchati)

g. **aśvau na vadataḥ**
(aśvau na vadataḥ)

h. **rāmas putram vadati**
(rāmaḥ putraṃ vadati)

5. Translate the following sentences into Sanskrit:

a. The men speak to the deer. (one deer)

b. Rāma speaks to the horses.

c. The son goes to the horse and stands.

d. Elephants do not remember.

e. Where are the horses standing?

f. Where is the elephant?

g. Rāma speaks and the son remembers.

h. They stand or they go.

i. Where does Rāma stand?

j. Rāma or the son goes.

k. Rāma and the son go.

6. Translate the following sentences into English:

   a. **narau putram vadataḥ**
   (narau putraṃ vadataḥ)

   b. **kutra aśvās ca gajās ca gacchanti**
   (kutra aśvāś ca gajāś ca gacchanti)

   c. **aśvas mṛgas vā gacchati**
   (aśvo mṛgo vā gacchati)

   d. **rāmas putrau vadati**
   (rāmaḥ putrau vadati)

   e. **mṛgas aśvas gajas ca gacchanti**
   (mṛgo 'śvo gajaś ca gacchanti)

   f. **putrās mṛgān na smaranti**
   (putrā mṛgān na smaranti)

   g. **kutra narau vasataḥ**
   (kutra narau vasataḥ)

   h. **rāmam pṛcchāmi**
   (rāmaṃ pṛcchāmi)

i. **narau putrān na vadataḥ**
(narau putrān na vadataḥ)

j. **kutra mṛgās bhavanti**
(kutra mṛgā bhavanti)

7. Translate the following sentences into Sanskrit:

a. Where is Rāma going?

b. Rāma is going to the horse.

c. The son does not speak to the horses.

d. The two elephants remember the man.

e. Where do the two deer live?

f. You go to the horse.

g. Where are we standing?

h. The son goes to the horses and the elephants.

i. You are all speaking to the elephant.

j. The elephant does not remember.

SUMMARY SHEET

	Singular	Dual	Plural
Third	**gacchati** (he, she goes)	**gacchataḥ** (they two go)	**gacchanti** (they all go)
Second	**gacchasi** (you go)	**gacchathaḥ** (you two go)	**gacchatha** (you all go)
First	**gacchāmi** (I go)	**gacchāvaḥ** (we two go)	**gacchāmaḥ** (we all go)

VERBS

√gam	**gacchati**	he goes
√prach	**pṛcchati**	he asks
√bhū	**bhavati**	he is
√vad	**vadati**	he speaks, he says
√vas	**vasati**	he lives
√sthā	**tiṣṭhati**	he stands
√smṛ	**smarati**	he remembers

NOUN STEMS

	Singular	Dual	Plural
Nominative (subject)	**naras**	**narau**	**narās**
Accusative (object)	**naram**	**narau**	**narān**

aśva horse

gaja elephant

nara man

putra son

mṛga deer

rāma Rāma

INDECLINABLES

kutra where

ca and

na not

vā or

5

LESSON FIVE

Alphabet: The rest of the alphabet in **devanāgarī**

Grammar: The instrumental and dative cases

Vocabulary: More nouns that end in short **a**

ALPHABET

1. Here are the last five stops:

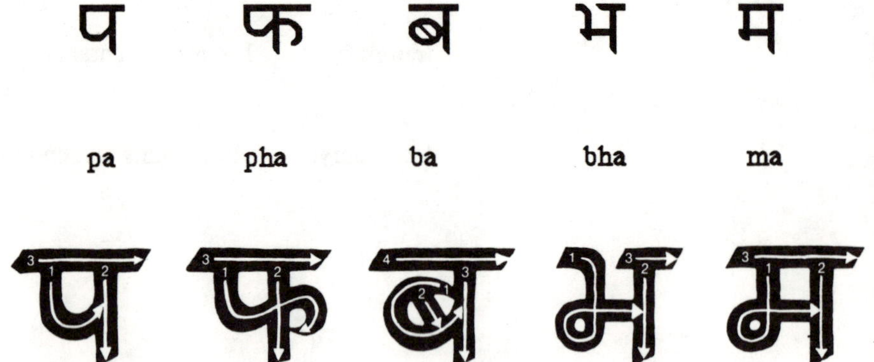

2. Here are the semi-vowels:

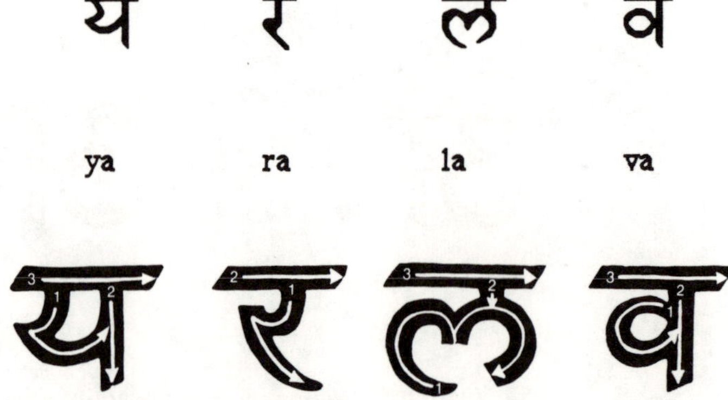

3. Here are the sibilants and aspirate:

4. Here is the **anusvāra** and **visarga** following **a**:

5. On the following page is the entire alphabet in **devanāgarī** script:

VOWELS	अ	a	आ	ā						
	इ	i	ई	ī						
	उ	u	ऊ	ū						
	ऋ	ṛ	ॠ	ṝ						
	ऌ	ḷ								
	ए	e	ऐ	ai						
	ओ	o	औ	au						
ANUSVĀRA	अं	aṃ (ṃ)								
VISARGA	अः	aḥ (ḥ)								
VELAR	क	ka	ख	kha	ग	ga	घ	gha	ङ	ṅa
PALATAL	च	ca	छ	cha	ज	ja	झ	jha	ञ	ña
RETROFLEX	ट	ṭa	ठ	ṭha	ड	ḍa	ढ	ḍha	ण	ṇa
DENTAL	त	ta	थ	tha	द	da	ध	dha	न	na
LABIAL	प	pa	फ	pha	ब	ba	भ	bha	म	ma
SEMI-VOWELS			य	ya	र	ra	ल	la	व	va
SIBILANTS			श	śa	ष	ṣa	स	sa	ह	ha

GRAMMAR: INSTRUMENTAL AND DATIVE

1. We will now learn two new cases, the instrumental (**tṛtīyā**) and the dative (**caturthī**).

2. The instrumental is used for accompaniment. For example:

   gajena saha rāmas gacchati (without **sandhi**)
   (**gajena saha rāmo gacchati**) (with **sandhi**)
   Rāma goes with the elephant.
   (instrumental)

   The word **saha** is often used after the instumental to indicate accompaniment.

3. The instrumental is also used to express instrumentality, or "by means of." (Although this usage is derived from the first, it is used more frequently.) For example:

   I write with a pen.
   (instrumental)

4. The dative is used for the indirect object. It shows "purpose." For example:

   rāmas putrāya aśvam gacchati (without **sandhi**)
   (**rāmaḥ putrāya aśvaṃ gacchati**) (with **sandhi**)
   Rāma goes to the horse for the son.
   (dative)

   rāmas putrāya pustakam paṭhati (without **sandhi**)
   (**rāmaḥ putrāya pustakaṃ paṭhati**) (with **sandhi**)
   Rāma reads the book to the son.
   (dative)

5. Here is how they are formed:

Stem: **nara** (masculine) man

	Singular	Dual	Plural
Instrumental	**nareṇa***	**narābhyām**	**narais**
Dative	**narāya**	**narābhyām**	**narebhyas**

*"With the elephant" is **gajena**

6. We will learn the following **sandhi** rule in more detail in Lesson 11. For now, when a word contains an **r** or **ṛ**, it often changes the following **n** to **ṇ**. For example: **nareṇa**, **putreṇa**, **mṛgeṇa**, **rāmeṇa**. But **aśvena**, **gajena**.

7. The word order is not rigid in Sanskrit. Usually the instrumental goes near the word most closely associated with it, and the dative goes before the verb. (More will be said about word order later.)

8. The verbs **vadati** (he says) and **pṛcchati** (he asks) often take a "double accusative": the object talked about and the person addressed. In this case, the context will give you the correct meaning. For example:

    rāmas mṛgam putram vadati (without **sandhi**)
    (**rāmo mṛgaṃ putraṃ vadati**) (with **sandhi**)
    Rāma speaks to the son about the deer.

VOCABULARY	SANSKRIT	ENGLISH
	tatra (indeclinable)	there
	nṛpa (mas)	king
	bāla (mas)	boy
	vīra (mas)	hero
	saha (indeclinable)	with (often used after the instrumental as a marker of accompaniment)

EXERCISES

1. Learn the alphabet in **devanāgarī**.

2. Learn the forms for the instrumental and dative. By now you have learned four cases.

3. Learn the vocabulary and keep up with all past vocabulary.

4. Translate the following sentences:

   a. **kutra vīrās tiṣṭhanti**
   (kutra vīrās tiṣṭhanti)

   b. **bālau gajena saha tatra bhavataḥ**
   (bālau gajena saha tatra bhavataḥ)

   c. **nṛpas aśvam gacchati**
   (nṛpo 'śvaṃ gacchati)

   d. **aśvena saha vīras nṛpān gacchati**
   (aśvena saha vīro nṛpān gacchati)

   e. **mṛgeṇa saha rāmas vasati**
   (mṛgeṇa saha rāmo vasati)

   f. **gajais saha bālās gacchanti**
   (gajaiḥ saha bālā gacchanti)

   g. **narās putram vadanti**
   (narāḥ putraṃ vadanti)

   h. **vīrās mṛgān rāmam pṛcchanti** (same as 5b. below)
   (vīrā mṛgān rāmaṃ pṛcchanti)

i. **tatra bālas nṛpāya gacchati**
(**tatra bālo nṛpāya gacchati**)

5. Translate the following sentences into Sanskrit:

a. The boys go to the horses.

b. The son asks the king about the deer. (double accusative)

c. The king remembers the man.

d. The hero lives with the son.

e. The boy asks the king and the king remembers.

f. There are no elephants with the son.

g. Where does Rāma live?

h. The king or the hero speaks to the boy.

i. The hero goes for the boy.

j. The elephants are there with the horses.

k. I remember the king.

l. You are going there with the boy.

6. Translate the following sentences into English:

a. **aśvais saha vīras gacchati**
(**aśvaiḥ saha vīro gacchati**)

b. **tatra nṛpāya narās gacchanti**
(tatra nṛpāya narā gacchanti)

c. **vīrau tiṣṭhataḥ vadataḥ ca**
(vīrau tiṣṭhato vadataś ca)

d. **mṛgās tatra vasanti**
(mṛgās tatra vasanti)

e. **kutra bālābhyām saha nṛpas gacchati**
(kutra bālābhyāṃ saha nṛpo gacchati)

f. **rāmas aśvam putram pṛcchati**
(rāmo 'śvaṃ putraṃ pṛcchati)

g. **tatra gajās na tiṣṭhanti**
(tatra gajā na tiṣṭhanti)

h. **vīras nṛpam bālam vadati**
(vīro nṛpaṃ bālaṃ vadati)

i. **mṛgais aśvais ca saha gajas vasati**
(mṛgair aśvaiś ca saha gajo vasati)

j. **kutra tiṣṭhāmaḥ**
(kutra tiṣṭhāmaḥ)

7. Translate the following sentences into Sanskrit:

a. The king lives there with the two boys.

b. Where are you going with the elephants?

c. The man goes there for the horse.

d. The boy does not remember the king.

e. I am speaking to the king about the two elephants.

f. The king goes to the horse for the son.

g. Where are we standing?

h. The man asks the boy about the horse.

i. Rāma goes there for the man.

j. Where are all the deer?

SUMMARY SHEET

Third	**gacchati** (he, she goes)	**gacchataḥ** (they two go)	**gacchanti** (they all go)
Second	**gacchasi** (you go)	**gacchathaḥ** (you two go)	**gacchatha** (you all go)
First	**gacchāmi** (I go)	**gacchāvaḥ** (we two go)	**gacchāmaḥ** (we all go)
	Singular	Dual	Plural

VERBS

√**gam**	**gacchati**	he goes
√**prach**	**pṛcchati**	he asks
√**bhū**	**bhavati**	he is
√**vad**	**vadati**	he speaks, he says
√**vas**	**vasati**	he lives
√**sthā**	**tiṣṭhati**	he stands
√**smṛ**	**smarati**	he remembers

NOUN STEMS

aśva	horse
gaja	elephant
nara	man
nṛpa	king
putra	son
bāla	boy
mṛga	deer
rāma	Rāma
vīra	hero

	Singular	Dual	Plural
Nominative (subject)	**naras**	**narau**	**narās**
Accusative (object)	**naram**	**narau**	**narān**
Instrumental (with)	**nareṇa***	**narābhyām**	**narais**
Dative (for)	**narāya**	**narābhyām**	**narebhyas**

***gajena, bālena** (See page 46.)

INDECLINABLES

kutra	where
ca	and
tatra	there
na	not
vā	or
saha	with (used after instrumental)

6

LESSON SIX

Alphabet: How vowels are formed when they follow consonants

Grammar: The ablative and the genitive
The use of **iti**

Vocabulary: More nouns in **a**

ALPHABET: VOWELS AFTER CONSONANTS

1. The vowel characters learned so far are used only when they are the first letter of a word. For example, **eka** (one) is written:

   एक **eka**

2. A consonant without a vowel following it is written with a short stroke (**virāma**) behind it. For example:

क	**ka**	प	**pa**
क्	**k**	प्	**p**

3. When a vowel follows a consonant, the vowel is written in contracted form. The **a** is replaced by other vowels. Here are the vowel forms:

ga	ग	gā	गा
gi	गि	gī	गी
gu	गु	gū	गू

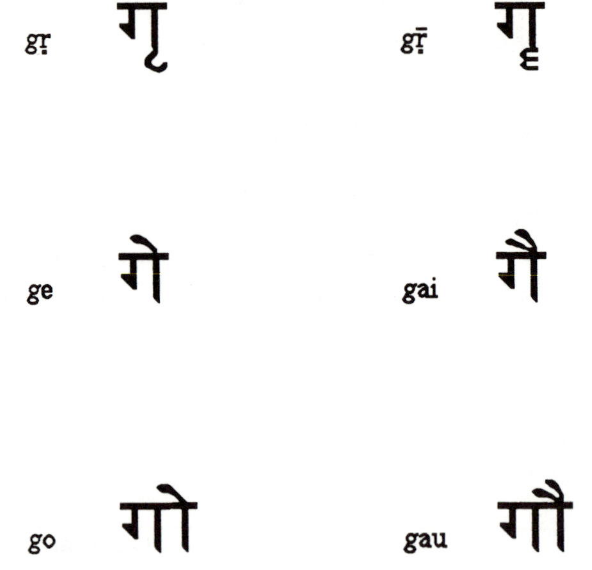

4. Note that the sign for the **i** is written before the consonant, even though the **i** is sounded after the consonant. When written by hand, the curved line on top should touch the vertical line of the consonant. For example: गि

5. These vowel signs may follow all consonants, including the semi-vowels, sibilants, and aspirate. For example:

च	चा	चि	ची	चु	चू	चृ	चॄ
ca	cā	ci	cī	cu	cū	cṛ	cṝ

चे	चै	चो	चौ
ce	cai	co	cau

ज	जा	जि	जी	जु	जू	जृ	जॄ
ja	jā	ji	jī	ju	jū	jṛ	jṝ
जे	जै	जो	जौ				
je	jai	jo	jau				
प	पा	पि	पी	पु	पू	पृ	पॄ
pa	pā	pi	pī	pu	pū	pṛ	pṝ
पे	पै	पो	पौ				
pe	pai	po	pau				

6. Sometimes these signs are put in different places. For example:

ru is written: रु

rū is written: रू

hṛ is written: हृ

We will learn more of these forms in the next lesson.

7. Words are formed by putting the letters together. For example:

गज	वीर	वसति
gaja	vīra	vasati

GRAMMAR: ABLATIVE AND GENITIVE

1. Now we will learn the ablative (**pañcamī**) and genitive (**ṣaṣṭhī**) cases (**vibhakti**).

2. The ablative is used for origin or source. It usually means "from." It is also used for comparison. For example:

   gajāt āgacchati
   (**gajād āgacchati**)
   He comes <u>from the elephant</u>.
   (ablative)

   One learns <u>from practice</u>. (ablative)
   He is taller <u>than her.</u> (ablative)

3. The genitive is used for possession. For example:

   narasya aśvas
   (**narasyāśvas**)
   the horse <u>of the man</u>.
   (genitive)

4. The genitive is always used in relation to the noun which follows it. For example:

   rāmasya putras the son of Rāma (or Rāma's son)
   (**rāmasya putraḥ**)

   amṛtasya putrās sons of immortality
   (**amṛtasya putrāḥ**)

5. The genitive is sometimes used as a substitute for other cases, such as the dative, instrumental, ablative, and locative.

6. Here is the formation of the ablative and genitive:

Stem: **nara** (masculine) man

	Singular	Dual	Plural
Ablative	**narāt**	**narābhyām**	**narebhyas**
Genitive	**narasya**	**narayos**	**narāṇām***

***gajānām, bālānām** (See page 46.)

7. Now we will learn the use of **iti**. This important particle is used at the end of a quotation. For example:

aśvas gacchati iti rāmas vadati
(**aśvo gacchatīti rāmo vadati**)
"The horse goes," says Rāma.

Notice that **iti** is a convenient point to break the sentence down into smaller, more manageable parts.

8. When translating from English to Sanskrit, indirect quotations must first be turned into direct quotations before **iti** can be used. For example:

He says that he is going. (indirect quotation)
"I am going," he says. (direct quotation)
gacchāmi iti vadati
(**gacchāmīti vadati**)

Notice that the change from an indirect quotation to a direct quotation changes the clause from "he is going" to "I am going."

VOCABULARY	SANSKRIT	ENGLISH
	atra (indeclinable)	here
	ā + √**gam** (root) **āgacchati**	he comes
	iti (indeclinable)	indicates the end of a quotation
	grāma (mas)	village
	hasta (mas)	hand

EXERCISES

1. Learn to recognize and write the **devanāgarī** for vowels that follow consonants.

2. Learn the forms for the ablative and genitive.

3. Write the following words in **devanāgarī**:

a.	**iti**	g.	**bhavāvaḥ**	m.	**ṛṣi**
b.	**nara**	h.	**vadasi**	n.	**devatā**
c.	**rāma**	i.	**nṛpas**	o.	**guṇa**
d.	**gaja**	j.	**na**	p.	**jaya**
e.	**vīra**	k.	**vā**	q.	**guru**
f.	**vasati**	l.	**ca**	r.	**deva**

4. Translate the following sentences into English, using the summary sheet:

   a. **bālasya gajas grāmam gacchati**
   (bālasya gajo grāmaṃ gacchati)

   b. **rāmasya putras aśvam gacchati**
   (rāmasya putro 'śvaṃ gacchati)

   c. **atra aśvas bhavati iti nṛpas vadati**
   (atrāśvo bhavatīti nṛpo vadati)

   d. **grāmāt putras āgacchati**
   (grāmāt putra āgacchati)

e. **kutra gajās tiṣṭhanti iti nṛpas pṛcchati**
(**kutra gajās tiṣṭhantīti nṛpaḥ pṛcchati**)

f. **bālas nṛpasya grāmam gacchati**
(**bālo nṛpasya grāmaṃ gacchati**)

g. **atra vīrās vasanti iti narās vadanti**
(**atra vīrā vasantīti narā vadanti**)

h. **kutra gacchasi iti rāmas pṛcchati**
(**kutra gacchasīti rāmaḥ pṛcchati**)

5. Translate the following sentences into Sanskrit:

a. "I live here," the son says.

b. The horses and elephants are coming from the village.

c. "Do you remember the men?" the king asks the boy.

d. Rāma says that he is going to the village.

e. "I am going to the village for the boy," says Rāma.

f. Where does the hero go?

g. "The hero goes to the village," says the king.

h. The son of the king lives here.

i. The king's sons come from the village.

j. The man speaks to Rāma about the elephants.

6. Translate the following sentences into English:

a. **narau grāmāt āgacchataḥ**
(**narau grāmād āgacchataḥ**)

b. **atra bhavāmi iti bālas nṛpam vadati**
(**atra bhavāmīti bālo nṛpaṃ vadati**)

c. **kutra vasasi iti vīras putram pṛcchati**
(**kutra vasasīti vīraḥ putraṃ pṛcchati**)

d. **rāmeṇa saha atra vasāmi iti putras vadati**
(**rāmeṇa sahātra vasāmīti putro vadati**)

e. **narasya putrās tatra tiṣṭhanti**
(**narasya putrās tatra tiṣṭhanti**)

f. **atra vīrasya hastau bhavataḥ**
(**atra vīrasya hastau bhavataḥ**)

g. **rāmam smarasi iti bālās naram pṛcchanti**
(**rāmaṃ smarasīti bālā naraṃ pṛcchanti**)

h. **kutra grāmas bhavati iti naras putram pṛcchati**
(**kutra grāmo bhavatīti naraḥ putraṃ pṛcchati**)

i. **grāmas tatra bhavati iti putras naram vadati**
(**grāmas tatra bhavatīti putro naraṃ vadati**)

j. **gajāya grāmam gacchāmi iti naras vadati**
(gajāya grāmaṃ gacchāmīti naro vadati)

7. Translate the following sentences into Sanskrit:

a. "Where are you going?" the king asks the boy.

b. "I am going to the horse," the boy says.

c. The king of the villages speaks to the men.

d. The two boys are coming from the horse and the elephant.

e. The boy lives with Rāma.

f. "Here are the sons of Rāma," says the hero.

g. The king says that the boys are standing there.

h. "I am going to the village," says the son of the hero.

i. The two horses are coming here with the two deer.

j. The king's hands are there.

SUMMARY SHEET

Third	**gacchati** (he, she goes)	**gacchataḥ** (they two go)	**gacchanti** (they all go)
Second	**gacchasi** (you go)	**gacchathaḥ** (you two go)	**gacchatha** (you all go)
First	**gacchāmi** (I go)	**gacchāvaḥ** (we two go)	**gacchāmaḥ** (we all go)
	Singular	Dual	Plural

VERBS

ā + √gam	**āgacchati**	he comes
√gam	**gacchati**	he goes
√prach	**pṛcchati**	he asks
√bhū	**bhavati**	he is
√vad	**vadati**	he speaks, he says
√vas	**vasati**	he lives
√sthā	**tiṣṭhati**	he stands
√smṛ	**smarati**	he remembers

NOUNS

aśva	horse
gaja	elephant
grāma	village
nara	man
nṛpa	king
putra	son
bāla	boy
mṛga	deer
rāma	Rāma
vīra	hero
hasta	hand

	Singular	Dual	Plural
Nom (subject)	**naras**	**narau**	**narās**
Acc (object)	**naram**	**narau**	**narān**
Inst (with)	**nareṇa***	**narābhyām**	**narais**
Dative (for)	**narāya**	**narābhyām**	**narebhyas**
Abl (from)	**narāt**	**narābhyām**	**narebhyas**
Gen (of, 's)	**narasya**	**narayos**	**narāṇām***

***gajena**, **gajānām** (See page 46.)

INDECLINABLES

atra	he
iti	end of quote
kutra	where
ca	and
tatra	there
na	not
vā	or
saha	with

7

LESSON SEVEN

Alphabet: Conjunct consonants

Grammar: The locative and vocative

Vocabulary: More nouns in **a**

ALPHABET: CONJUNCT CONSONANTS

1. We will now learn how to write two or more consonants without a vowel coming between them. To write **tva**, remove the vertical line from the **t**. For example:

tava तव

tva त्व

2. Here are examples of other clusters of consonants that are written side by side:

tma	त्म	ṣya	ष्य
sya	स्य	tya	त्य
bhya	भ्य	nta	न्त
nti	न्ति	ṣṭa	ष्ट

3. Some clusters are written on top of each other. For example:

dva	द्व	dda	द्द
ṅga	ङ्ग	ddho	द्धो

4. Consonant conjuncts are read left to right and top to bottom. They will be learned most easily by close observation to their formation as we continue with the exercises.

5. When the semi-vowel **r** comes immediately before another consonant, the **r** takes the form of a small hook above the consonant. For example:

rpa	र्प	**rmya**	र्म्य
ryā	र्या	**rgo**	र्गो

Notice that the **r** is placed as far to the right as possible.

6. When **r** immediately follows a consonant, the **r** takes the form of a small slanted stroke, written near the bottom of the vertical line (**daṇḍa**, meaning "stick"), if there is a vertical line. For example:

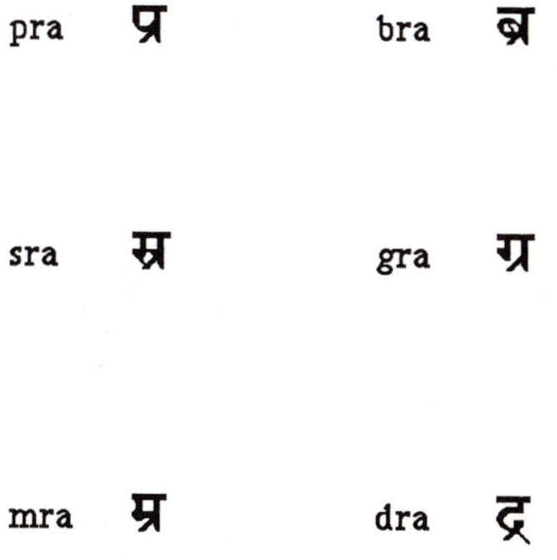

pra प्र
bra ब्र
sra स्र
gra ग्र
mra म्र
dra द्र

7. Some forms are completely different than the two letters that make them up. These must be learned:

tra	त्र	**jña**	ज्ञ		
kṣa	क्ष	**śva**	श्व	(or)	श्‍व
kta	क्त	(or)	क्‍त		
tta	त्त	**dya**	द्य		
hma	ह्म	**hya**	ह्य		

8. A vertical line (**daṇḍa**) is used as a period at the end of a sentence. It is also used to mark the halfway part of a verse. Two vertical lines mark the end of a paragraph or the end of a verse. For example:

रामस् गच्छति ।

9. There are other ways of forming certain letters, which you should be able to recognize:

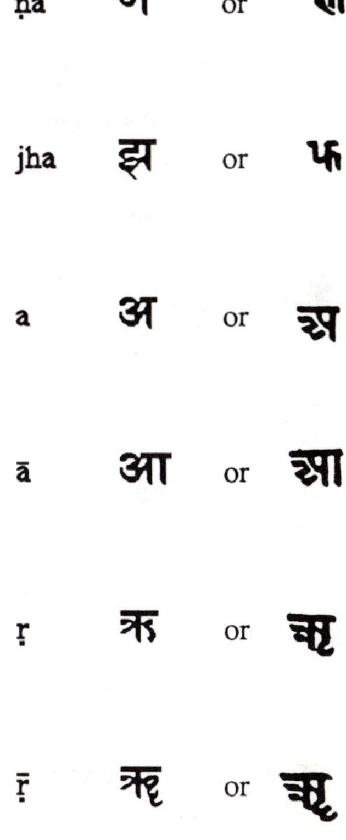

GRAMMAR: LOCATIVE AND VOCATIVE

1. Now we will learn the locative (**saptamī**) and vocative (**saṃbodhana**—"awakening," "arousing").

2. The locative case is used to express location. For example:

grāme vasati	**gaje tiṣṭhati** (same with **sandhi**)
He lives in the village.	He stands on the elephant.
(locative)	(locative)

3. The vocative is used for address. The vocative often, but not always, begins a sentence. For example:

rāma atra āgacchasi
(**rāma atrāgacchasi**)
Oh Rāma, you are coming here.
(vocative)

Indian grammarians do not consider the vocative a true case (**vibhakti**) like the seven other cases, but a modification of the nominative, or naming case.

4. Here is the formation of the locative and vocative:

stem: **nara** (masculine) man

	Singular	Dual	Plural
Locative	**nare**	**narayos**	**nareṣu**
Vocative	**nara**	**narau**	**narās**

5. Like verbs, there is a parsing code, or way of classifying nouns. They are classified according to:

Gender (**liṅga**):	Masculine (**puṃ-liṅga**)	(mas)
	Feminine (**strī-liṅga**)	(fem)
	Neuter (**napuṃsaka-liṅga**)	(n)
Case (**vibhakti**):	Nominative (**prathamā**)	(nom)
	Accusative (**dvitīyā**)	(acc)
	Instrumental (**tṛtīyā**)	(inst)
	Dative (**caturthī**)	(dat)
	Ablative (**pañcamī**)	(abl)
	Genitive (**ṣaṣṭhī**)	(gen)
	Locative (**saptamī**)	(loc)
	Vocative (**saṃbodhana**)	(voc)
Number (**vacana**):	Singular (**eka-vacana**)	(sing)
	Dual (**dvi-vacana**)	(dual)
	Plural (**bahu-vacana**)	(pl)

6. The word **naras** would be classified as masculine, nominative, singular. Its parsing code would be mas, nom, sing.

   The word **narān** would be classified as masculine, accusative, plural. Its parsing code would be mas, acc, pl.

7. Here is the entire short **a** masculine declension:

Stem: **nara** (masculine) man

	Singular	Dual	Plural
Nominative (subject)	नरस् **naras**	नरौ **narau**	नरास् **narās**
Accusative (object)	नरम् **naram**	नरौ **narau**	नरान् **narān**
Instrumental (with)	नरेण **nareṇa***	नराभ्याम् **narābhyām**	नरैस् **narais**
Dative (for)	नराय **narāya**	नराभ्याम् **narābhyām**	नरेभ्यस् **narebhyas**
Ablative (from)	नरात् **narāt**	नराभ्याम् **narābhyām**	नरेभ्यस् **narebhyas**
Genitive (of, 's)	नरस्य **narasya**	नरयोस् **narayos**	नराणाम् **narāṇām***
Locative (in, on)	नरे **nare**	नरयोस् **narayos**	नरेषु **nareṣu**
Vocative (Oh)	नर **nara**	नरौ **narau**	नरास् **narās**

*gajena, gajānām (See p. 46.)

VOCABULARY

SANSKRIT		ENGLISH
आचार्य	**ācārya** (mas)	teacher
चन्द्र	**candra** (mas)	moon
चिन्त्	√**cint** (root) **cintayati**	he thinks
पश्	√**paś** (root) **paśyati** (√**dṛś** is also considered to be the root.)	he sees
विना	**vinā** (indeclinable)	without (used like **saha**)
शिष्य	**śiṣya** (mas)	student
सूर्य	**sūrya** (mas)	sun

EXERCISES

1. Learn the examples given for consonant conjuncts. Put these words into roman letters (transliterate them):

   a. पुराण
   b. गन्धर्व
   c. छन्दस्
   d. व्याकरण
   e. गच्छति
   f. चन्द्र
   g. ज्योतिष
   h. कल्प
   i. अश्व
   j. पुत्रस्य
   k. शिष्यस्
   l. तिष्ठन्ति

2. Learn the forms for the locative and vocative.

3. Parse the following words and give their meaning:

   a. **narās**
   b. **hastau**
   c. **bālānām**
   d. **nṛpāt**
   e. **rāmāya**
   f. **mṛgeṇa**
   g. **gajais**
   h. **vīrān**
   i. **grāmeṣu**
   j. **ācāryāya**

4. Translate the following sentences into English. (Use the summary sheet.) Cover the **devanāgarī** with a sheet of paper, write it yourself, and then compare:

a. शिष्यस् चन्द्रम् सूर्यम् च पश्यति ।

śiṣyas candram sūryam ca paśyati
(śiṣyaś candraṃ sūryaṃ ca paśyati)

b. राम गजास् ग्रामे तिष्ठन्ति ।

rāma gajās grāme tiṣṭhanti
(rāma gajā grāme tiṣṭhanti)

c. वीरस् ग्रामे वसति इति आचार्यस् शिष्यम् वदति ।

vīras grāme vasati iti ācāryas śiṣyam vadati
(vīro grāme vasatīty ācāryaḥ śiṣyaṃ vadati)

d. कुत्र चन्द्रस् भवति इति पुत्रस् पृच्छति ।

kutra candras bhavati iti putras pṛcchati
(kutra candro bhavatīti putraḥ pṛcchati)

e. तत्र गजे बालौ तिष्ठतः ।

tatra gaje bālau tiṣṭhataḥ
(tatra gaje bālau tiṣṭhataḥ)

f. पुत्र कुत्र चन्द्रस् भवति इति वीरस् बालम् पृच्छति ।

putra kutra candras bhavati iti vīras bālam pṛcchati
(putra kutra candro bhavatīti vīro bālaṃ pṛcchati)

g. आचार्यस्य शिष्यस् तिष्ठति वदति च ।

ācāryasya śiṣyas tiṣṭhati vadati ca
(ācāryasya śiṣyas tiṣṭhati vadati ca)

h. रामेण विना वीरास् ग्रामात् आगच्छन्ति ।

rāmeṇa vinā vīrās grāmāt āgacchanti
(rāmeṇa vinā vīrā grāmād āgacchanti)

i. ग्रामे वसामि इति वीरस्य बालस् चिन्तयति ।

grāme vasāmi iti vīrasya bālas cintayati
(grāme vasāmīti vīrasya bālaś cintayati)

5. Translate the following sentences into Sanskrit:

a. The king tells the hero that the boys are going to the village.

b. Without the king, the boys come.

c. In the hand of the hero is the son.

d. "Where am I?" thinks the boy.

e. He asks the son of the hero where the men are.

f. The teacher tells the student that the sun is not the moon.

g. The king lives in the village.

h. There are the elephants of the king.

6. Translate the following sentences into English:

a. रामेण विना बालस् ग्रामम् गच्छति ।
rāmeṇa vinā bālas grāmam gacchati
(rāmeṇa vinā bālo grāmaṃ gacchati)

b. कुत्र नृपस्य गजास् भवन्ति ।
kutra nṛpasya gajās bhavanti
(kutra nṛpasya gajā bhavanti)

c. अत्र भवामि इति बालस् नरम् वदति ।
atra bhavāmi iti bālas naram vadati
(atra bhavāmīti bālo naraṃ vadati)

d. सूर्येण विना चन्द्रम् न पश्यसि ।

sūryeṇa vinā candram na paśyasi

(sūryeṇa vinā candraṃ na paśyasi)

e. आचार्यस् शिष्यान् वदति ।

ācāryas śiṣyān vadati

(ācāryaḥ śiṣyān vadati)

f. चन्द्रम् पश्यामि इति बालस् चिन्तयति ।

candram paśyāmi iti bālas cintayati

(candraṃ paśyāmīti bālaś cintayati)

g. अत्र ग्रामाणाम् नृपस् आगच्छति ।

atra grāmāṇām nṛpas āgacchati

(atra grāmāṇāṃ nṛpa āgacchati)

h. नृपस् वीरस्य हस्तौ पश्यति ।

nṛpas vīrasya hastau paśyati

(nṛpo vīrasya hastau paśyati)

i. कुत्र सूर्यस् चन्द्रस् च भवतः इति बालस् पृच्छति ।

kutra sūryas candras ca bhavataḥ iti bālas pṛcchati

(kutra sūryaś candraś ca bhavata iti bālaḥ pṛcchati)

j. शिष्यास् नरम् न स्मरन्ति ।

śiṣyās naram na smaranti

(śiṣyā naraṃ na smaranti)

7. Translate the following sentences into Sanskrit, writing first in roman script and then in **devanāgarī**:

   a. "Where are you going?" the boy asks the king's son.

   b. The two deer are in the village.

   c. The teacher speaks to the hero's son.

   d. The king sees the sun and the moon.

   e. Without the sun we do not see the moon.

   f. The hero is on the elephant of the king.

g. "We live in the villages," the boys say.

h. Rāma goes from the horses to the elephants.

i. "Where are we going?" the boy asks the king.

j. The teacher lives in the village with the students.

8. Transliterate the following:

1. ऋषि
2. आसन
3. अहंकार
4. गुण
5. ज्ञान
6. कुरुक्षेत्र
7. कर्म
8. ध्यान
9. दर्शन
10. दुःख
11. वेद्
12. चित्त
13. चित्तवृत्ति
14. अविद्या
15. अव्यक्त
16. धारण
17. आत्मन्
18. आनन्द्
19. अष्टाङ्गयोग
20. तत्त्वमसि
21. नामरूप
22. उपनिषद्
23. नित्य
24. धर्म

SUMMARY SHEET

Third	**gacchati** (he, she goes)	**gacchataḥ** (they two go)	**gacchanti** (they all go)
Second	**gacchasi** (you go)	**gacchathaḥ** (you two go)	**gacchatha** (you all go)
First	**gacchāmi** (I go)	**gacchāvaḥ** (we two go)	**gacchāmaḥ** (we all go)
	Singular	Dual	Plural

VERBS

ā + √gam	**āgacchati**	he comes
√gam	**gacchati**	he goes
√cint	**cintayati**	he thinks
√paś (**√dṛś**)	**paśyati**	he sees
√prach	**pṛcchati**	he asks
√bhū	**bhavati**	he is
√vad	**vadati**	he speaks, he says
√vas	**vasati**	he lives
√sthā	**tiṣṭhati**	he stands
√smṛ	**smarati**	he remembers

NOUN STEMS

aśva	horse
ācārya	teacher
gaja	elephant
grāma	village
candra	moon
nara	man
nṛpa	king
putra	son
bāla	boy
mṛga	deer
rāma	Rāma
vīra	hero
śiṣya	student
sūrya	sun
hasta	hand

	Singular	Dual	Plural
Nom (subject)	**naras**	**narau**	**narās**
Acc (object)	**naram**	**narau**	**narān**
Inst (with)	**nareṇa***	**narābhyām**	**narais**
Dat (for)	**narāya**	**narābhyām**	**narebhyas**
Abl (from)	**narāt**	**narābhyām**	**narebhyas**
Gen (of, 's)	**narasya**	**narayos**	**narāṇām***
Loc (in, on)	**nare**	**narayos**	**nareṣu**
Voc (Oh)	**nara**	**narau**	**narās**

***gajena**, **gajānām** (See page 46.)

INDECLINABLES

atra	he
iti	end of quote
kutra	where
ca	and
tatra	there
na	not
vā	or
vinā	without (used like **saha**)
saha	with

8

LESSON EIGHT

Alphabet: The **sandhi** rules for combining vowels

Grammar: Neuter nouns in short **a**

Vocabulary: Neuter nouns

ALPHABET: VOWEL SANDHI

1. The word **sandhi** means "combination" or "junction point." The rules of **sandhi** insure that sounds will combine in a pleasing, euphonic way. **Pāṇini** (1.4.109) also refers to these junction points as **saṃhitā**, or "togetherness." There are two types of **sandhi** rules:

    a. External **sandhi**, or changes at the junction between words
    b. Internal **sandhi**, or changes within a word

2. The **sandhi** rules involve sound changes so that the flow of the language is smooth. As mentioned in Lesson 2, "an apple" is smoother to pronounce than "a apple." "The house" is pronounced differently than "the other house." These are examples of external **sandhi**. The **sandhi** rules of Sanskrit exist because the Sanskrit tradition has been primarily an oral tradition, and because its grammatical insights were so sophisticated. (The term **sandhi** has been adopted by modern linguists to describe sound modifications between words in any language.)

3. Don't allow the **sandhi** rules to overwhelm you. There are many rules to learn, but with practice you will gradually assimilate them. We will begin our study of the **sandhi** rules using charts, and then after we have used the rules for some time, we will memorize them. There will be three charts, because **sandhi** can be divided into three groups:

    a. Vowel **sandhi** (**svara-sandhi**) Lesson Eight
    b. Final **s sandhi** (**visarga-sandhi**) Lesson Nine
    c. Consonant **sandhi** (**hal-sandhi**) Lesson Ten

4. The chart on page 89 describes what happens if a word ends with a vowel and the next word begins with a vowel. For example, if one word ends with a short **i**, and the next word begins with an **a**, then the two combine (**sandhi**) to form **ya**:

गच्छति + **अश्वम्** would be written **गच्छत्यश्वम्**

gacchati + aśvam would be written **gacchaty aśvam**

एव + **अवशिष्यते** = **एवावशिष्यते**

eva + avaśiṣyate = evāvaśiṣyate

ब्रह्म + **अस्मि** = **ब्रह्मास्मि**

brahma + asmi = brahmāsmi

भव + **अर्जुन** = **भवार्जुन**

bhava + arjuna = bhavārjuna

5. On the following page is the chart describing the **sandhi** change if the first word ends in a vowel (the vowels at the top of the chart) and the second word begins in a vowel (the vowels in the right column). If a vowel has ˘̄ above it, then it refers to a short or a long vowel.

6. This chart need not be memorized. It should be used in the exercises, and the rules will be memorized later, once the patterns of change are more clear.

FINAL VOWELS							INITIAL VOWELS
ā̆	ī̆	ū̆	ṛ	e	ai	au	
ā	ya	va	ra	e '	ā a	āva	a
ā	yā	vā	rā	a ā	ā ā	āvā	ā
e	ī	vī̆	rī̆	a ī̆	ā ī̆	āvī̆	ī̆
o	yū̆	ū	rū̆	a ū̆	ā ū̆	āvū̆	ū̆
ar	yṛ	vṛ	ṝ	a ṛ	ā ṛ	āvṛ	ṛ
ai	ye	ve	re	a e	ā e	āve	e
ai	yai	vai	rai	a ai	ā ai	āvai	ai
au	yo	vo	ro	a o	ā o	āvo	o
au	yau	vau	rau	a au	ā au	āvau	au

7. Here are some examples:

i + ū = yū

ṛ + i = ri

i + u = yu

गच्छति + इति = गच्छतीति

gacchati + iti = gacchatīti

8. The apostrophe ('), written in **devanāgarī** by **ऽ**, represents the missing letter **a**. It is called **avagraha**, meaning "separation." For example:

ग्रामे + अत्र = ग्रामे ऽत्र

grāme + atra = grāme 'tra

9. Once the **sandhi** rules have been applied, there is no further application of **sandhi** rules. The **sandhi** rules are only applied once.

10. In this text, words are always separated in transliteration (roman script), unless two vowels have formed one long vowel, such as **i** + **i** = **ī**. In **devanāgarī** script, words involving vowel **sandhi** are joined except when there is a space (hiatus) between the vowels in the chart. Until you learn more **sandhi** rules, all other words should be kept separated. For example:

गच्छति + इति = गच्छतीति

gacchati + iti = gacchatīti

गच्छति + अश्वम् = गच्छत्यश्वम्

gacchati + aśvam = gacchaty aśvam

11. In vowel **sandhi**, often a vowel will be replaced by the semi-vowel that corresponds to it (**samprasāraṇa**). For example, **i** will be replaced by **y**. In English, similar changes occur, such as the change from "lady" to "ladies." This table need not be memorized; it is just for observation:

	Vowels	Semi-vowels
Palatal	**i , ī**	**y**
Retroflex	**ṛ , ṝ**	**r**
Dental	**ḷ**	**l**
Labial	**u , ū**	**v**

12. Some vowels (**pragṛhya**) are not subject to **sandhi**. They are:

    a. The vowels **i**, **u**, and **e** when they are dual endings.

    b. The final vowel of an interjection. For example, **rāma āgacchanti** (Rāma, they come.) needs no **sandhi**.

13. The rules for this lesson are written out in Lesson 13. We will memorize them at that time.

GRAMMAR: NEUTER NOUNS

1. All the nouns that we have studied so far have been masculine. Now we will study the neuter nouns that end in short **a**. The neuter nouns decline like the masculine nouns, except in the nominative, accusative, and vocative.

2. Here is the formation of the neuter short **a** nouns:
   Stem: **phala** (neuter) fruit

	Singular	Dual	Plural
Nominative	फलम् phalam	फले phale	फलानि phalāni
Accusative	फलम् phalam	फले phale	फलानि phalāni
Instrumental	फलेन phalena	फलाभ्याम् phalābhyām	फलैस् phalais
Dative	फलाय phalāya	फलाभ्याम् phalābhyām	फलेभ्यस् phalebhyas
Ablative	फलात् phalāt	फलाभ्याम् phalābhyām	फलेभ्यस् phalebhyas
Genitive	फलस्य phalasya	फलयोस् phalayos	फलानाम् phalānām
Locative	फले phale	फलयोस् phalayos	फलेषु phaleṣu
Vocative	फल phala	फले phale	फलानि phalāni

VOCABULARY

SANSKRIT		ENGLISH
अमृतम्	**amṛtam** (neuter)	immortality, an immortal
कथम्	**katham** (indeclinable)	how (used like **kutra**)
ज्ञानम्	**jñānam** (neuter)	knowledge
पठ्	√**paṭh** (root) **paṭhati**	he reads
पुस्तकम्	**pustakam** (neuter)	book
फलम्	**phalam** (neuter)	fruit
वनम्	**vanam** (neuter)	forest
शास्त्रम्	**śāstram** (neuter)	scripture
सत्यम्	**satyam** (neuter)	truth
सूक्तम्	**sūktam** (neuter)	hymn

In order to remember the difference between masculine and neuter nouns, in the vocabulary neuter nouns are given in their nominative singular form, instead of the stem, which is the same short **a** as the masculine.

EXERCISES

1. We had learned that a **ṛ** or **r** changes the following **n** to **ṇ**. This change will not occur if a **t** comes between, because the **t** changes the position of the tongue. Therefore: **amṛtāni**, **amṛtena**, **amṛtānām**. But: **śāstrāṇi**, **śātreṇa**, **śāstrāṇām**. This **sandhi** rule will be studied in more detail in Lesson 11.

2. Put the following words together, using correct **sandhi** rules, and then put the final form in **devanāgarī**:

a.	**putreṇa atra**	f.	**devau āgacchataḥ**
b.	**saha ācāryas**	g.	**nare atra**
c.	**tatra iti**	h.	**vane iti**
d.	**iti atra**	i.	**phalāni iti**
e.	**iti ācāryas**	j.	**smarati atra**

3. Write in roman script and take out the **sandhi**:

a.	गच्छतीति	f.	नृपस्याश्वस्
b.	गजावागच्छतः	g.	अश्वे ऽत्र
c.	पृच्छत्यागच्छति च	h.	कुत्राश्वस्
d.	गच्छामीति	i.	कुत्रेति
e.	हस्त इति	j.	गच्छत्यत्र

4. In the following exercises, remember that the subject and the predicate are put in the nominative case, since they both refer to the same subject. (See page 33.) For example:

   rāmas putras bhavati
   (rāmaḥ putro bhavati)
   Rāma is the son.

   In this text, the predicate is placed after the subject, although other word orders are equally common. (See 5b, c; 6a, f, g.)

5. In the the following sentences, cover up the roman script and transliterate each sentence (write in roman script). Then cover the **devanāgarī** and write in **devanāgarī**. Then take out any **sandhi**. Only the **sandhi** rules learned so far have been applied; that is, only when one word ends in a vowel and the next word begins in a vowel. Finally, translate into English:

   a. रामस् ग्रामात् वनम् गच्छति ।
   rāmas grāmāt vanam gacchati
   (rāmo grāmād vanaṃ gacchati)

   b. अमृतम् ज्ञानस्य फलम् भवति ।
   amṛtam jñānasya phalam bhavati
   (amṛtaṃ jñānasya phalaṃ bhavati)

   c. ज्ञानम् सत्यम् भवतीति बालास् शास्त्रे पठन्ति ।
   jñānam satyam bhavatīti bālās śāstre paṭhanti
   (jñānaṃ satyaṃ bhavatīti bālāḥ śāstre paṭhanti)

d. अमृतस्य पुत्रास् भवथेत्याचार्यस् शिष्यान् वदति ।
amṛtasya putrās bhavathety ācāryas śiṣyān vadati
(amṛtasya putrā bhavathety ācāryaḥ śiṣyān vadati)

e. कथम् आचार्यास् सूक्तानि स्मरन्ति ।
katham ācāryās sūktāni smaranti
(katham ācāryāḥ sūktāni smaranti)

f. शास्त्रेषु सत्यम् पश्यामीति रामस् वदति ।
śāstreṣu satyam paśyāmīti rāmas vadati
(śāstreṣu satyaṃ paśyāmīti rāmo vadati)

g. कुत्र सूक्तानाम् ज्ञानम् भवतीति वीरस् पुत्रम् पृच्छति ।
kutra sūktānām jñānam bhavatīti vīras putram pṛcchati
(kutra sūktānāṃ jñānaṃ bhavatīti vīraḥ putraṃ pṛcchati)

h. नृपस् बालाय पुस्तकम् पठति ।
nṛpas bālāya pustakam paṭhati
(nṛpo bālāya pustakaṃ paṭhati)

6. Translate the following sentences into Sanskrit. First write them without **sandhi**, then with (vowel) **sandhi**, and finally in **devanāgarī**.

   a. The elephant is not the king of the forest.

   b. How do you see the moon?

   c. Rāma thinks that he sees the deer.

   d. The fruit is in the hands of the boy.

   e. How does the king live without Rāma?

   f. Rāma is the king.

   g. The king is Rāma.

   h. The hero lives in the village of the immortals.

7. Translate the following sentences into English. First write in roman script, then take out the **sandhi**, and finally write in English:

   a. कथम् सूर्येण विना नरास् नृपम् पश्यन्ति ।

   (कथं सूर्येण विना नरा नृपं पश्यन्ति ।)

   b. शिष्यानाम् आचार्यस् पुस्तकम् पठति ।

   (शिष्यानामाचार्यः पुस्तकं पठति ।)

c. अत्र वने फलानि भवन्तीति बालस् वीरम् वदति ।

(अत्र वने फलानि भवन्तीति बालो वीरं वदति ।)

d. मृगस् वने वसति गजस् च ग्रामे वसति ।

(मृगो वने वसति गजश्च ग्रामे वसति ।)

(When a phrase or clause is joined by **ca**, it takes the second position. See p. 28.)

e. ज्ञानम् पुस्तके न भवतीत्याचार्यस् वदति ।

(ज्ञानं पुस्तके न भवतीत्याचार्यो वदति ।)

f. पुस्तकेन विना शिष्यस् ज्ञानम् स्मरति ।

(पुस्तकेन विना शिष्यो ज्ञानं स्मरति ।)

g. राम कुत्र मृगेण सह गच्छसीति पुत्रस् पृच्छति ।

(राम कुत्र मृगेण सह गच्छसीति पुत्रः पृच्छति ।)

h. नृपस् बालाय पुस्तकम् पठति ।

(नृपो बालाय पुस्तकं पठति ।)

8. Translate the following sentences into Sanskrit. Translate, put in the vowel **sandhi**, and write in **devanāgarī**:

   a. Where do you read the knowledge of immortality?

   b. How does Rāma go to the forest without the horses?

   c. "The hymns are in the book," the teacher tells the students.

   d. Rāma sees the truth and speaks the truth.

   e. "I see the sun and the moon," says the son of the king.

   f. Without knowledge, there are no teachers or students.

   g. The hero speaks to the boys about immortality.

   h. The horses, elephants, and boys come from the village.

9. Transliterate the following:

1. पुराण	13. रामराज्य
2. राम	14. रामायण
3. पुरुष	15. शिष्य
4. प्रकृति	16. स्थितप्रज्ञ
5. प्रज्ञा	17. भगवद्गीता
6. सीता	18. समाधि
7. सुखम्	19. शङ्कर
8. संयम	20. बुद्ध
9. संसार	21. महाभारत
10. संस्कार	22. प्रज्ञापराध
11. संस्कृत	23. वेदान्त
12. सत्यम्	24. वेदलीला

SUMMARY SHEET

Third	**gacchati** (he, she goes)	**gacchataḥ** (they two go)	**gacchanti** (they all go)
Second	**gacchasi** (you go)	**gacchathaḥ** (you two go)	**gacchatha** (you all go)
First	**gacchāmi** (I go)	**gacchāvaḥ** (we two go)	**gacchāmaḥ** (we all go)
	Singular	Dual	Plural

VERBS

ā + √gam	**āgacchati**	he comes
√gam	**gacchati**	he goes
√cint	**cintayati**	he thinks
√paṭh	**paṭhati**	he reads
√paś (**√dṛś**)	**paśyati**	he sees
√prach	**pṛcchati**	he asks
√bhū	**bhavati**	he is
√vad	**vadati**	he speaks, he says
√vas	**vasati**	he lives
√sthā	**tiṣṭhati**	he stands
√smṛ	**smarati**	he remembers

MASCULINE NOUNS

	Singular	Dual	Plural
Nom (subject)	**naras**	**narau**	**narās**
Acc (object)	**naram**	**narau**	**narān**
Inst (with)	**nareṇa***	**narābhyām**	**narais**
Dat (for)	**narāya**	**narābhyām**	**narebhyas**
Abl (from)	**narāt**	**narābhyām**	**narebhyas**
Gen (of, 's)	**narasya**	**narayos**	**narāṇām***
Loc (in, on)	**nare**	**narayos**	**nareṣu**
Voc (Oh)	**nara**	**narau**	**narās**

*__gajena__, __gajānām__ (See page 46.)

MASCULINE NOUN STEMS

aśva	horse	**śiṣya**	student
ācārya	teacher	**sūrya**	sun
gaja	elephant	**hasta**	hand
grāma	village		
candra	moon		
nara	man		
nṛpa	king		
putra	son		
bāla	boy		
mṛga	deer		
rāma	Rāma		
vīra	hero		

NEUTER NOUNS

	Singular	Dual	Plural
Nom (subject)	**phalam**	**phale**	**phalāni***
Acc (object)	**phalam**	**phale**	**phalāni***
Inst (with)	**phalena***	**phalābhyām**	**phalais**
Dat (for)	**phalāya**	**phalābhyām**	**phalebhyas**
Abl (from)	**phalāt**	**phalābhyām**	**phalebhyas**
Gen (of, 's)	**phalasya**	**phalayos**	**phalānām***
Loc (in, on)	**phale**	**phalayos**	**phaleṣu**
Voc (Oh)	**phala**	**phale**	**phalāni***

***śāstrāṇi**, **śāstreṇa**, **śāstrāṇām**

NEUTER NOUNS

(given in nominative form)

amṛtam	immortality
jñānam	knowledge
pustakam	book
phalam	fruit
vanam	forest
śāstram	scripture
satyam	truth
sūktam	hymn

INDECLINABLES

atra	here
iti	end of quote
katham	how (used like **kutra**)
kutra	where
ca	and
tatra	there
na	not
vā	or
vinā	without
saha	with

THE MONKEY AND THE CROCODILE

Translate the following, using the vocabulary on the next page. Words not given you should already know.

1. तत्र गङ्गायाम् कुम्भीरस् भवति ।

   (तत्र गङ्गायां कुम्भीरो भवति ।)

2. वानरस् तटे वसति ।

   (वानरस्तटे वसति ।)

3. वानरस् फलानि कुम्भीराय निक्षिपति ।

   (वानरः फलानि कुम्भीराय निक्षिपति ।)

4. कुम्भीरस् फलानि खादति ।

   (कुम्भीरः फलानि खादति ।)

5. भार्या वानरस्य हृदयम् इच्छति ।

   (भार्या वानरस्य हृदयमिच्छति ।)

6. हृदयम् वृक्षे भवतीति वानरस् वदति ।

   (हृदयं वृक्षे भवतीति वानरो वदति ।)

7. कश्चित् हृदयम् चोरयतीति वानरस् वदति ।
(कश्चिद्धृदयं चोरयतीति वानरो वदति ।)

8. एवम् कुम्भीरस् वानरस् च मित्रे तिष्ठतः ।
(एवं कुम्भीरो वानरश्च मित्रे तिष्ठतः ।)

VOCABULARY (IN ORDER OF APPEARANCE)

1. **gaṅgā** (fem noun) Ganges. This follows the feminine declension for long **ā**. The locative is **gaṅgāyām**, "in the Ganges."
   kumbhīra (mas noun) crocodile.

2. **vānara** (mas noun) monkey.
   taṭa (mas noun) bank (of the river).

3. **nikṣipati** (3rd per sing verb) throws down.

4. **khādati** (3rd per sing verb) eats.

5. **bhāryā** (fem noun) wife. This, again, follows the feminine declension for long **ā**. The stem, as well as the nominative, is **bhāryā**.
   hṛdayam (neuter noun) heart. The **ṛ** is written next to the **h**. (See Lesson 6, page 57.)
   icchati (3rd per sing verb) wants (to eat).

6. **vṛkṣa** (mas noun) tree.

7. **kaś cit** (ind) someone.
   corayati (3rd per sing verb) steals.

8. **evaṁ** (ind) therefore.
   mitram (neuter noun) friend. (Here it is used in the nom dual.)
   tiṣṭhati (3rd per sing verb) remain, or stand as. (Here used in the dual.)

   (The story will become more clear when it is studied in detail in Lesson 11.)

9

LESSON NINE

Aphabet: The **sandhi** rules for final **s**

Grammar: The middle voice and "have"

Vocabulary: Verbs in the middle voice

ALPHABET: SANDHI RULES FOR FINAL S

1. The following chart describes the changes that take place when the first word ends in **s**. There are three categories: **as**, **ās**, and **s** preceded by any other vowel:

FINAL LETTERS OF FIRST WORD:

Any vowel **s** or **r** (except **as** and **ās**)	**ās**	**as**	INITIAL LETTER OF SECOND WORD:	
r	ā	a [(2)]	vowels	(a)
r	ā	o	g/gh	
r	ā	o	j/jh	
r	ā	o	ḍ/ḍh	
r	ā	o	d/dh	(b)
r	ā	o	b/bh	
r	ā	o	nasals (n/m)	
r	ā	o	y/v	
– [(1)]	ā	o	r	
r	ā	o	l	
r	ā	o	h	
ḥ	āḥ	aḥ	k/kh	
ś	āś	aś	c/ch	
ṣ	āṣ	aṣ	ṭ/ṭh	
s	ās	as	t/th	
ḥ	āḥ	aḥ	p/ph	(c)
ḥ	āḥ	aḥ	ś	
ḥ	āḥ	aḥ	ṣ/s	
ḥ	āḥ	aḥ	end of line	

(1) The **s** disappears, and if **i** or **u** precedes, it becomes **ī** or **ū**.

The **r** disappears, and if **a**, **i**, or **u** precedes, it becomes **ā**, **ī**, or **ū**.

(2) Except that **as** + **a** = **o '** For example:

रामस् + अत्र = रामो ऽत्र

rāmas + atra = rāmo 'tra

2. If the first word ends in **as**, then use the third column. If the first word ends in **ās**, then use the middle column. If the first word ends in any other vowel before the **s**, then use the first column.

3. Here are some examples:

Without **sandhi**	With **sandhi**
रामस् गच्छति **rāmas gacchati**	रामो गच्छति **rāmo gacchati**
वीरास् गच्छन्ति **vīrās gacchanti**	वीरा गच्छन्ति **vīrā gacchanti**
रामस् पश्यति **rāmas paśyati**	रामः पश्यति **rāmaḥ paśyati**
वीरास् पश्यन्ति **vīrās paśyanti**	वीराः पश्यन्ति **vīrāḥ paśyanti**

4. Before **sandhi**, final **ḥ** (as in **gacchataḥ**) should be treated as an **s**.

5. After these **sandhi** rules have been applied, if the first word ends in a vowel or **ḥ**, then there is a break between words in **devanāgarī**. For now, words that do not follow these **sandhi**

rules should be kept separate. In this text, when writing in roman script, words are usually separated, unless the **sandhi** change is a result of two vowels joining together, such as **bhavārjuna**. For example:

Without **sandhi**	With **sandhi**
रामस् चिन्तयति **rāmas cintayati**	रामश्चिन्तयति **rāmaś cintayati**
रामस् तिष्ठति **rāmas tiṣṭhati**	रामस्तिष्ठति **rāmas tiṣṭhati**
गच्छति इति **gacchati iti**	गच्छतीति **gacchatīti**
भव अर्जुन **bhava arjuna**	भवार्जुन **bhavārjuna**

6. Notice that the chart is divided into three groups on the right side: (a), (b), and (c). These three groups are determined by the first letter of the second word. The groups are:

   (a) Vowels
   (b) Voiced consonants
   (c) Unvoiced consonants (The end of the line is considered to be unvoiced.)

7. The following chart (described in more detail in Lesson 14) puts the **sandhi** changes into these three groups. It gives the same information as the first chart, but in a more conceptual form, so that later on it will be easier to memorize. Each group represents the first letter of the second word:

a	**ā**	
i	**ī**	
u	**ū**	(a)
ṛ	**ṝ**	Vowels
ḷ		
e	**ai**	
o	**au**	

ḥ		**ka**	**kha**	|	**ga**	**gha**	**ṅa**	
ś		**ca**	**cha**	|	**ja**	**jha**	**ña**	
ṣ		**ṭa**	**ṭha**	|	**ḍa**	**ḍha**	**ṇa**	
s		**ta**	**tha**	|	**da**	**dha**	**na**	
ḥ		**pa**	**pha**	|	**ba**	**bha**	**ma**	
				|	**ya**	**ra**	**la**	**va**
ḥ	**śa**	**ṣa**	**sa**	|	**ha**			
ḥ	end of line			|				
	(c) Unvoiced consonant			|	(b) Voiced consonant			

(a) If the second word begins in a vowel:

as becomes **a** (except **as** + **a** = **o '**)

ās becomes **ā**

vowel **s** becomes **r**

(b) If the first letter of the second word is a voiced consonant:

as becomes **o**

ās becomes **ā**

vowel **s** becomes **r** (except before a word beginning in **r**)

(c) If the first letter of the second word is an unvoiced consonant, the **s** changes to the letter in the far left column.

GRAMMAR: MIDDLE VERBS

1. Now we will learn the middle endings (**ātmane-pada**). For the middle voice, the fruit of action is said to go to the agent (**ātman**). For the active voice, the fruit of action goes to someone else (**para**). Many verbs take both endings, some take active endings only, and a few take middle endings only.

2. Here is the formation of the middle verb √**bhāṣ** (to speak):

	Singular	Dual	Plural
third	**bhāṣate**	**bhāṣete**	**bhāṣante**
second	**bhāṣase**	**bhāṣethe**	**bhāṣadhve**
first	**bhāṣe**	**bhāṣāvahe**	**bhāṣāmahe**

3. Although most of the verbs we have learned (before √**bhāṣ**) are seen more often with active endings, they could take middle endings also (in situations where the fruit of action goes more to the agent). These verbs are listed in the dictionary like this: √**gam gacchati -te**, indicating that the first ending (**-ti**) is more common, but the second (**-te**) is sometimes used. Verbs listed with only one ending always take that ending.

4. There is no verb for "have" in Sanskrit. "Have" is formed with the genitive and √**bhū**. For example:

वीरस्य पुत्रो भवति ।

vīrasya putro bhavati

Of the hero a son is. (becomes)

The hero has a son.

VOCABULARY

SANSKRIT		ENGLISH
एव	**eva** (ind)	only, ever
गृहम्	**gṛham** (neuter)	house
जलम्	**jalam** (neuter)	water
जि	√**ji** (active) **jayati -te**	he conquers
दुःखम्	**duḥkham*** (neuter)	suffering
भाष्	√**bhāṣ** (middle) **bhāṣate -ti**	he speaks
मन्	√**man** (middle) **manyate -ti**	he thinks
लभ्	√**labh** (middle) **labhate -ti**	he obtains
सुखम्	**sukham** (neuter)	happiness
सेव्	√**sev** (middle) **sevate -ti**	he serves

*When the **ḥ** occurs in the middle of a word, it is pronounced as a strong breath of air. When **ḥ** is before a **k** or **kh**, it is sometimes called **jihvāmūlīya**. When it is before **p** or **ph**, it is sometimes called **upadhmānīya**.

EXERCISES

1. Put in the correct **sandhi** for the following phrases:

a. रामस् गच्छति

b. बालास् आगच्छन्ति

c. वीरौ आगच्छतः

d. शिष्यस् अत्र

e. रामस् इति

f. देवास् स्मरन्ति

g. पुत्रस् पश्यति

h. अश्वस् वदति

2. Take out the **sandhi** in the following phrases:

a. रामो गच्छति

b. कुत्रागच्छसि

c. सूर्यश्चन्द्रश्च

d. गजैर्वीरः

e. अश्वा आगच्छन्ति

f. रामः पुत्रश्च

g. गजैः सह

h. फलयोर्जलम्

3. Translate the following sentences into English. Take out the **sandhi** (for vowels and final **s**), and then translate:

a. वीरस्य बालो भवति ।

vīrasya bālo bhavati

(वीरस्य बालो भवति ।)

b. सुखम् ज्ञानस्य फलम् भवति ।

sukham jñānasya phalam bhavati

(सुखं ज्ञानस्य फलं भवति ।)

c. शिष्या गृहात् जलम् आचार्याय लभन्ते ।

śiṣyā gṛhāt jalam ācāryāya labhante

(शिष्या गृहाज्जलमाचार्याय लभन्ते ।)

d. रामस्तत्र जलाय गच्छतीति वीरो वदति ।

rāmas tatra jalāya gacchatīti vīro vadati

(रामस्तत्र जलाय गच्छतीति वीरो वदति ।)

e. शिष्य आचार्यम् सेवते ।

śiṣya ācāryam sevate

(शिष्य आचार्यं सेवते ।)

f. शिष्या ज्ञानम् आचार्यात् लभन्ते ।

śiṣyā jñānam ācāryāt labhante

(शिष्या ज्ञानमाचार्याल्लभन्ते ।)

g. राम कथम् दुःखम् जयसि ।

rāma katham duḥkham jayasi

(राम कथं दुःखं जयसि ।)

h. पुत्रो गृहात् नृपस्याश्वेषु गच्छति ।

putro gṛhāt nṛpasyāśveṣu gacchati

(पुत्रो गृहान्नृपस्याश्वेषु गच्छति ।)

i. अमृतम् सुखस्य फलम् भवत इति मन्यते ।

amṛtam sukhasya phalam bhavata iti manyate

(अमृतं सुखस्य फलं भवत इति मन्यते ।)

j. आचार्यो ज्ञानस्य पुस्तकम् शिष्याय पठति ।

ācāryo jñānasya pustakam śiṣyāya paṭhati

(आचार्यो ज्ञानस्य पुस्तकं शिष्याय पठति ।)

4. Translate the following sentences into Sanskrit. First write in roman, then **devanāgarī**, and then write again with the (vowel and final **s**) **sandhi**:

   a. The water is in Rāma's hands.

   b. The boy reads the book.

   c. The hero stands ever in the house of the king.

   d. The boys obtain the fruits from the forest.

   e. "You conquer suffering with knowledge," the teacher says.

   f. From the fruit the boy obtains water. (Use singular for "fruit.")

   g. "I see truth in the sun and the moon," says Rāma.

   h. Without knowledge there is suffering.

   i. "I do not come from the village," the king's son says.

   j. The hero and the boy live in the forest.

SUMMARY SHEET

Third	**gacchati** (he, she goes)	**gacchataḥ** (they two go)	**gacchanti** (they all go)
Second	**gacchasi** (you go)	**gacchathaḥ** (you two go)	**gacchatha** (you all go)
First	**gacchāmi** (I go)	**gacchāvaḥ** (we two go)	**gacchāmaḥ** (we all go)
	Singular	Dual	Plural

VERBS PRIMARILY TAKING ACTIVE ENDINGS

ā + √gam	**āgacchati**	he comes
√gam	**gacchati -te**	he goes
√cint	**cintayati -te**	he thinks
√ji	**jayati -te**	he conquers
√paṭh	**paṭhati -te**	he reads
√paś (√dṛś)	**paśyati -te**	he sees
√prach	**pṛcchati -te**	he asks
√bhū	**bhavati -te**	he is
√vad	**vadati -te**	he speaks, he says
√vas	**vasati -te**	he lives
√sthā	**tiṣṭhati -te**	he stands
√smṛ	**smarati -te**	he remembers

MIDDLE ENDINGS

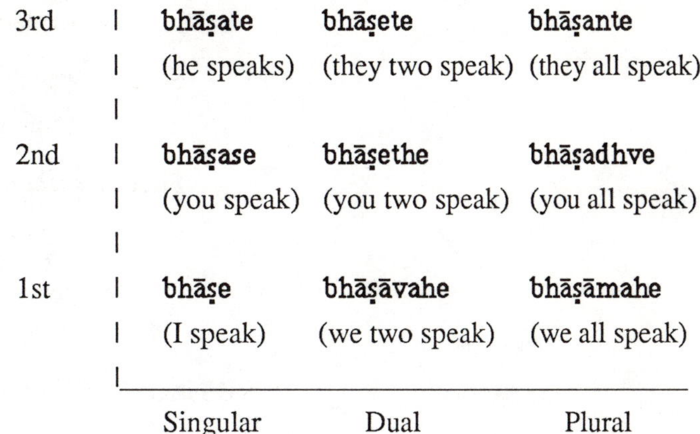

	Singular	Dual	Plural
3rd	**bhāṣate** (he speaks)	**bhāṣete** (they two speak)	**bhāṣante** (they all speak)
2nd	**bhāṣase** (you speak)	**bhāṣethe** (you two speak)	**bhāṣadhve** (you all speak)
1st	**bhāṣe** (I speak)	**bhāṣāvahe** (we two speak)	**bhāṣāmahe** (we all speak)

VERBS PRIMARILY TAKING MIDDLE ENDINGS

√**bhāṣ**	**bhāṣate -ti**	he speaks
√**man**	**manyate -ti**	he thinks
√**labh**	**labhate -ti**	he obtains
√**sev**	**sevate -ti**	he serves

MASCULINE NOUNS

	Singular	Dual	Plural
Nom (subject)	**naras**	**narau**	**narās**
Acc (object)	**naram**	**narau**	**narān**
Inst (with)	**nareṇa***	**narābhyām**	**narais**
Dat (for)	**narāya**	**narābhyām**	**narebhyas**
Abl (from)	**narāt**	**narābhyām**	**narebhyas**
Gen (of, 's)	**narasya**	**narayos**	**narāṇām***
Loc (in, on)	**nare**	**narayos**	**nareṣu**
Voc (Oh)	**nara**	**narau**	**narās**

***gajena, gajānām** (See page 46.)

MASCULINE NOUN STEMS

aśva	horse	**vīra**	hero
ācārya	teacher	**śiṣya**	student
gaja	elephant	**sūrya**	sun
grāma	village	**hasta**	hand
candra	moon		
nara	man		
nṛpa	king		
putra	son		
bāla	boy		
mṛga	deer		
rāma	Rāma		

NEUTER NOUNS

	Singular	Dual	Plural
Nom (subject)	**phalam**	**phale**	**phalāni****
Acc (object)	**phalam**	**phale**	**phalāni****
Inst (with)	**phalena****	**phalābhyām**	**phalais**
Dat (for)	**phalāya**	**phalābhyām**	**phalebhyas**
Abl (from)	**phalāt**	**phalābhyām**	**phalebhyas**
Gen (of, 's)	**phalasya**	**phalayos**	**phalānām****
Loc (in, on)	**phale**	**phalayos**	**phaleṣu**
Voc (Oh)	**phala**	**phale**	**phalāni****

***śāstrāṇi, śāstreṇa, śāstrāṇām**

NEUTER NOUNS (given in nominative form)

amṛtam	immortality	**satyam**	truth
gṛham	house	**sukham**	happiness
jalam	water	**sūktam**	hymn
jñānam	knowledge		
duḥkham	suffering		
pustakam	book		
phalam	fruit		
vanam	forest		
śāstram	scripture		

INDECLINABLES

atra	here
iti	end of quote
eva	only, ever
katham	how (used like **kutra**)
kutra	where
ca	and
tatra	there
na	not
vā	or
vinā	without
saha	with

RĀMĀYAṆA

Translate the following, using the vocabulary given afterward:

रामायणम् ।

1. अयोध्यायाम् दशरथो नाम नृपो वसति ।

   (अयोध्यायां दशरथो नाम नृपो वसति ।)

2. दशरथस्य चत्वारः पुत्रा भवन्ति ।

   (दशरथस्य चत्वारः पुत्रा भवन्ति ।)

3. पुत्रा रामो भरतो लक्ष्मणः शत्रुघ्नो भवन्ति ।

   (पुत्रा रामो भरतो लक्ष्मणः शत्रुघ्नो भवन्ति ।)

4. रामः सुन्दरः शान्तो वीरश्च भवति ।

   (रामः सुन्दरः शान्तो वीरश्च भवति ।)

5. नृपो रामे स्निह्यति ।

   (नृपो रामे स्निह्यति ।)

6. रामो मिथिलाम् लक्ष्मणेन सह गच्छति ।

   (रामो मिथिलां लक्ष्मणेन सह गच्छति ।)

7. तत्र रामः सीताम् पश्यति ।

(तत्र रामः सीतां पश्यति ।)

8. सीतायाम् स्निह्यामीति रामो वदति ॥

(सीतायां स्निह्यामीति रामो वदति ॥)

VOCABULARY

1. **ayodhyā** (fem) the city of Ayodhyā. (The locative is **ayodhyāyām**, "in Ayodhyā.")
   daśaratha (mas noun) Daśaratha, the king of Ayodhyā.
   nāma (ind) by name.

2. **catvāras** (nom) four. (used as an adjective)

3. **bharata, lakṣmaṇa, śatrughna** names of Rāma's brothers.

4. **sundara** (adjective) beautiful.
   śānta (adjective) peaceful.
   vīra strong. (here an adjective—strong like a hero)

5. **snihyati** he loves. (used with locative)

6. **mithilā** (fem) village of Mithilā. (The accusative is **mithilām**.)

7. **sītā** (fem) Sītā. (The accusative is **sītām**.)

8. The locative of **sītā** is **sītāyām**.

10

LESSON TEN

Alphabet: The remaining **sandhi** rules

Grammar: Pronouns and adjectives
The verb √**as**

Vocabulary: Adjectives and particles

ALPHABET: REMAINING SANDHI RULES

1. Here is the chart for the **sandhi** rules for final **t**, **n**, and **m**:

FINAL LETTER OF FIRST WORD: t	n	m	INITIAL LETTER OF SECOND WORD:
d	n[1]	m	vowels
d	n	ṃ	g/gh
j	ñ	ṃ	j/jh
ḍ	ṇ	ṃ	ḍ/ḍh
d	n	ṃ	d/dh
d	n	ṃ	b/bh
n	n	ṃ	nasals (n/m)
d	n	ṃ	y/v
d	n	ṃ	r
l	ṃl	ṃ	l
d(dh)[3]	n	ṃ	h
t	n	ṃ	k/kh
c	ṃś	ṃ	c/ch
ṭ	ṃṣ	ṃ	ṭ/ṭh
t	ṃs	ṃ	t/th
t	n	ṃ	p/ph
c(ch)[4]	ñ (ch)[2]	ṃ	ś
t	n	ṃ	ṣ/s
t	n	m	end of line

1. If the vowel before the **n** is short, the **n** becomes **nn**.

2. The following **ś** may become **ch**.

3. The following **h** becomes **dh**.

4. The following **ś** becomes **ch**.

2. Many of the changes on this chart occur because the last letter of the first word is "getting ready" to say the first letter of the next word. This rule, which often involves a change of voicing, is called "regressive assimilation." The prior sound is assimilated.

3. There are a few additional rules, which are used less often. They are discussed in Lesson 18.

4. There are no **sandhi** changes and there is a space between words if the first word ends in a vowel and the second word begins with a consonant.

5. At one time the manuscripts didn't have any breaks between words, sentences, or paragraphs in the written script. Fortunately, modern editions have introduced some spaces between words. Words are separated in **devanāgarī** as much as possible without changing how they are written or without adding a **virāma**.

6. Here are the cases that result in a break between words. With vowel **sandhi**, the breaks in **devanāgarī** are shown by the chart. In the last two charts, there is a break in the **devanāgarī** between the words with any **sandhi** change that results in the first word ending in a vowel, ḥ, or ṃ:

   रामस् गच्छति = रामो गच्छति (vowel)

   रामस् पृच्छति = रामः पृच्छति (ḥ)

   रामम् गच्छामि = रामं गच्छामि (ṃ)

   rāmas gacchati = rāmo gacchati (vowel)
   rāmas pṛcchati = rāmaḥ pṛcchati (ḥ)
   rāmam gacchāmi = rāmaṃ gacchāmi (ṃ)

GRAMMAR: PRONOUNS AND ADJECTIVES

1. Pronouns (**sarva-nāman**) decline exactly the same way that nouns decline. This table is not, however, the endings, but the entire first person pronoun (I, we two, we, etc.):

   Stems: **mad** (singular) I; **asmad** (plural) we. Both are any gender.

		Singular	Dual	Plural
I, we	Nom	अहम् aham	आवाम् āvām	वयम् vayam
me, us	Acc	माम् मा mām (mā)	आवाम् नौ āvām (nau)	अस्मान् नस् asmān (nas)
with me, us	Inst	मया mayā	आवाभ्याम् āvābhyām	अस्माभिस् asmābhis
for me, us	Dat	मह्यम् मे mahyam (me)	आवाभ्याम् नौ āvābhyām (nau)	अस्मभ्यम् नस् asmabhyam (nas)
from me, us	Abl	मत् mat	आवाभ्याम् āvābhyām	अस्मत् asmat
of me, us my, our	Gen	मम मे mama (me)	आवयोस् नौ āvayos (nau)	अस्माकम् asmākam (nas)
on me, us	Loc	मयि mayi	आवयोस् āvayos	अस्मासु asmāsu

2. The Sanskrit words in parentheses are sometimes used. For example, **mā** is sometimes used instead of **mām** (except beginning a sentence).

3. Here is the second person pronoun (you):

Stems: **tvat** (singular) you; **yuṣmad** (plural) you. Both are any gender.

		Singular	Dual	Plural
you	Nom	त्वम् **tvam**	युवाम् **yuvām**	यूयम् **yūyam**
you	Acc	त्वाम् त्वा **tvām (tvā)**	युवाम् वाम् **yuvām (vām)**	युष्मान् वस् **yuṣmān (vas)**
with you	Inst	त्वया **tvayā**	युवाभ्याम् **yuvābhyām**	युष्माभिस् **yuṣmābhis**
for you	Dat	तुभ्यम् ते **tubhyam (te)**	युवाभ्याम् वाम् **yuvābhyām (vām)**	युष्मभ्यम् वस् **yuṣmabhyam (vas)**
from you	Abl	त्वत् **tvat**	युवाभ्याम् **yuvābhyām**	युष्मत् **yuṣmat**
of you / your	Gen	तव ते **tava (te)**	युवयोस् वाम् **yuvayos (vām)**	युष्माकम् वस् **yuṣmākam (vas)**
on you	Loc	त्वयि **tvayi**	युवयोस् **yuvayos**	युष्मासु **yuṣmāsu**

4. Adjectives (**viśeṣaṇa**) are considered nominals (**subanta**), or noun forms. They are declined like nouns. They are usually placed before the noun that they modify and agree with it in number, case, and gender. For example, the adjective for "beautiful" is **sundara**:

सुन्दरो गजो गच्छति ।

sundaro gajo gacchati (with **sandhi**)

The beautiful elephant goes.

If a genitive is also modifying a noun, the genitive goes closest to the noun. For example:

सुन्दरो नृपस्य गजो गच्छति ।

sundaro nṛpasya gajo gacchati (with **sandhi**)

The beautiful elephant of the king goes.

सुन्दरस्य नृपस्य गजो गच्छति ।

sundarasya nṛpasya gajo gacchati (with **sandhi**)

The elephant of the beautiful king goes.

5. The most common root in Sanskrit is √**as**, which means "to be." We have had another root, √**bhū**, which also means "to be," but √**as** is more common. It is used to mean "there is" and as a copula. For example:

There is the horse.	अश्वो ऽस्ति **aśvo 'sti**
Rāma is the king.	रामो नृपो ऽस्ति **rāmo nṛpo 'sti**

6. Here is the present indicative (**laṭ**) for √**as**. These are not the endings, but the entire verb:

Third	अस्ति **asti**	स्तः **staḥ**	सन्ति **santi**
Second	असि **asi**	स्थः **sthaḥ**	स्थ **stha**
First	अस्मि **asmi**	स्वः **svaḥ**	स्मः **smaḥ**
	Singular	Dual	Plural

Note how closely this is related to the endings for the active verbs. Note also that the singular forms begin with **a**, and the dual and plural begin with **s**.

7. This verb is often understood. That is, the verb is meant, but is not written in the sentence. For example:

रामो नृपो ऽस्ति ।	or	रामो नृपः ।
rāmo nṛpo 'sti	or	**rāmo nṛpaḥ**
Rāma is the king.		Rāma is the king.

8. Often this verb begins the sentence. For example:

अस्ति नृपो दशरथो ग्रामे ।

asti nṛpo daśaratho grāme

There is a king, Daśaratha, in the village.

VOCABULARY	SANSKRIT		ENGLISH
	अतीव	**atīva** (ind)	very
	अपि	**api** (ind)	also, too (placed after the word it modifies)
	अस्	√**as** (root) **asti** (3rd per sing)	he, she, or it is
	अस्मद्	**asmad** (plural)	we
	अहो	**aho** (ind)	aha! hey!
	एवम्	**evam** (ind)	thus, in this way
	कुपित	**kupita** (adj)	angry
	त्वद्	**tvad** (sing)	you
	धार्मिक	**dhārmika** (adj)	virtuous
	नाम	**nāma** (ind)	by name (placed after)
	पुनर्	**punar** (ind)	again
	भीत	**bhīta** (adj)	afraid
	मद्	**mad** (sing)	I
	युष्मद्	**yuṣmad** (plural)	you
	सुन्दर	**sundara** (adj)	beautiful

EXERCISES

1. Put in the correct **sandhi**, write in **devanāgarī**, and translate:

   a. **mama putras gacchati**

   b. **tava gajas mat tvām gacchati**

   c. **mama hastau pustakeṣu staḥ**

   d. **aham nṛpas asmi**

   e. **vayam aśve tiṣṭhāmaḥ**

   f. **tvam mama pustakam paṭhasi**

   g. **rāmas tava nṛpas asti**

   h. **yūyam gṛhe stha**

   i. **asmākam nṛpas kupitas asti**

   j. **tvayā saha aham gacchāmi**

   k. **dhārmikasya nṛpasya bhītas asti**

   l. **tvam sundaras**

2. Take out the **sandhi** and translate the following:

   a. नृपस्य पुत्रो ऽस्ति ।

b. अहो रामः पुनर्वदते ।

c. अहमतीव भीतो भवामि ।

d. आचार्या अपि पुस्तकानि पठन्ति ।

e. अस्ति नृपो रामो नाम वने ।

f. कथं तव गृहं गच्छामीति शिष्यः पृच्छति ।

g. वीरो मम ग्रामं जयति ।

h. पुत्रः सुन्दरात्फलाज्जलं लभते ।

i. सुखेन विना दुःखमस्ति ।

j. गजः सुन्दर इति पुत्रो मन्यते ।

3. Translate the following sentences, writing them first without **sandhi** (in **devanāgarī**) and then with **sandhi** (in **devanāgarī**):

   a. The student is not afraid of the teacher. (Use ablative for teacher.)

b. You obtain knowledge from the scriptures.

c. "The boy is there," says the hero to the teacher.

d. I ask the teacher about the deer.

e. "Where are you going?" the boy asks.

f. Again the hero comes to my house.

g. Your teacher speaks the truth.

h. Our horses are standing in the village.

i. There is a king, Rāma by name, in our village.

j. How do I obtain the king's horses from you?

SUMMARY SHEET

	Singular	Dual	Plural
Third	**gacchati** (he, she goes)	**gacchataḥ** (they two go)	**gacchanti** (they all go)
Second	**gacchasi** (you go)	**gacchathaḥ** (you two go)	**gacchatha** (you all go)
First	**gacchāmi** (I go)	**gacchāvaḥ** (we two go)	**gacchāmaḥ** (we all go)

VERBS PRIMARILY TAKING ACTIVE ENDINGS

ā + √gam	**āgacchati**	he comes
√gam	**gacchati -te**	he goes
√cint	**cintayati -te**	he thinks
√ji	**jayati -te**	he conquers
√paṭh	**paṭhati -te**	he reads
√paś (**√dṛś**)	**paśyati -te**	he sees
√prach	**pṛcchati -te**	he asks
√bhū	**bhavati -te**	he is
√vad	**vadati -te**	he speaks, he says
√vas	**vasati -te**	he lives
√sthā	**tiṣṭhati -te**	he stands
√smṛ	**smarati -te**	he remembers

	Sing	Dual	Plural
3rd	**bhāṣate** (he speaks)	**bhāṣete** (they two speak)	**bhāṣante** (they all speak)
2nd	**bhāṣase** (you speak)	**bhāṣethe** (you two speak)	**bhāṣadhve** (you all speak)
1st	**bhāṣe** (I speak)	**bhāṣāvahe** (we two speak)	**bhāṣāmahe** (we all speak)

VERBS PRIMARILY TAKING MIDDLE ENDINGS

√**bhāṣ**	**bhāṣate -ti**	he speaks
√**man**	**manyate -ti**	he thinks
√**labh**	**labhate -ti**	he obtains
√**sev**	**sevate -ti**	he serves

THE VERB √**as**

	Singular	Dual	Plural
3rd	**asti**	**staḥ**	**santi**
2nd	**asi**	**sthaḥ**	**stha**
1st	**asmi**	**svaḥ**	**smaḥ**

Charts for pronouns are listed on pages 307-311.

MASCULINE NOUNS

	Singular	Dual	Plural
Nom (subject)	**naras**	**narau**	**narās**
Acc (object)	**naram**	**narau**	**narān**
Inst (with)	**nareṇa***	**narābhyām**	**narais**
Dat (for)	**narāya**	**narābhyām**	**narebhyas**
Abl (from)	**narāt**	**narābhyām**	**narebhyas**
Gen (of, 's)	**narasya**	**narayos**	**narāṇām***
Loc (in, on)	**nare**	**narayos**	**nareṣu**
Voc (Oh)	**nara**	**narau**	**narās**

*__gajena__, **gajānām** (See page 46.)

MASCULINE NOUN STEMS

aśva	horse	**vīra**	hero
ācārya	teacher	**śiṣya**	student
gaja	elephant	**sūrya**	sun
grāma	village	**hasta**	hand
candra	moon		
nara	man		
nṛpa	king		
putra	son		
bāla	boy		
mṛga	deer		
rāma	Rāma		

NEUTER NOUNS

	Singular	Dual	Plural
Nom (subject)	**phalam**	**phale**	**phalāni***
Acc (object)	**phalam**	**phale**	**phalāni***
Inst (with)	**phalena***	**phalābhyām**	**phalais**
Dat (for)	**phalāya**	**phalābhyām**	**phalebhyas**
Abl (from)	**phalāt**	**phalābhyām**	**phalebhyas**
Gen (of, 's)	**phalasya**	**phalayos**	**phalānām***
Loc (in, on)	**phale**	**phalayos**	**phaleṣu**
Voc (Oh)	**phala**	**phale**	**phalāni***

***śāstrāṇi, śāstreṇa, śāstrāṇām**

NEUTER NOUNS (given in nominative form)

amṛtam	immortality	**satyam**	truth
gṛham	house	**sukham**	happiness
jalam	water	**sūktam**	hymn
jñānam	knowledge		
duḥkham	suffering		
pustakam	book		
phalam	fruit		
vanam	forest		
śāstram	scripture		

ADJECTIVES

kupita	angry
dhārmika	virtuous
bhīta	afraid
sundara	beautiful

INDECLINABLES

atīva	very
atra	here
api	also, too (placed after)
aho	aha! hey!
iti	end of quote
eva	only, ever
evam	thus, in this way
katham	how
kutra	where
ca	and
tatra	there
na	not
nāma	by name (placed after)
punar	again
vā	or
vinā	without
saha	with

11

LESSON ELEVEN

Alphabet: Internal **sandhi** rules

Grammar: Feminine nouns in **ā** and third person pronouns

Vocabulary: Feminine nouns

ALPHABET: INTERNAL SANDHI

1. We will learn only two internal **sandhi** rules at this time. These need not be memorized, but are mainly for recognition.

2. The first rule is that **s** changes to **ṣ** if preceded by any vowel but **a** or **ā**, or preceded by **k** or **r**. The rule does not apply if the **s** is final or followed by an **r**. It applies even if an **anusvāra** (**ṃ**) or **visarga** (**ḥ**) comes between the vowel, **k**, or **r**—and the **s**. This rule is clearer in chart form:

any vowel (but **a** or **ā**), **k**, or **r**	in spite of intervening **ṃ** or **ḥ**	changes **s** to **ṣ**	unless final or followed by **r**

3. If the following sound is **t**, **th**, or **n**, it is also retroflexed. For example:

sthā becomes **tiṣṭhati**

4. The second rule is that **n** changes to **ṇ** if preceded in the same word by **r**, **ṛ**, **ṝ**, or **ṣ**. Certain sounds may interrupt the process. Study this chart:

r **ṛ** or **ṣ**	unless **c**, **ch**, **j**, **jh**, **ñ**, **ṭ**, **ṭh**, **ḍ**, **ḍh**, **ṇ**, **t**, **th**, **d**, **dh**, **l**, **ś**, **s** interferes	changes **n** to **ṇ**	if followed by vowels, **m**, **y**, **v**, or **n**

5. Retroflex sounds, such as **r**, **ṛ**, **ṝ**, and **ṣ**, leave the tongue in a retroflexed position. Unless certain sounds interfere, such as retroflex sounds of the releasing type, like **ṭ**, or sounds from the row above or below, then **n** becomes retroflexed. For example:

   rāmeṇa (The **r** changes the **n** to **ṇ**.)
   putreṇa (The **r** changes the **n** to **ṇ**.)
   putrāṇām (The **r** changes the **n** to **ṇ**.)

6. If another **n** follows the **n**, they both become **ṇṇ**.

GRAMMAR: NOUNS IN Ā, THIRD PERSON PRONOUNS

1. There are standard endings to nouns, and it will help for learning all future declensions to learn the normal endings. Most declensions follow these endings much more closely than declensions ending in **a**. Notice that they are the same for all genders, except the neuter nominative and accusative:

	mas	fem	n	mas	fem	n	mas	fem	n
Nom	**s**	**s**	**m**	**au**	**au**	**ī**	**as**	**as**	**i**
Acc	**am**	**am**	**m**	**au**	**au**	**ī**	**as**	**as**	**i**
Inst	**ā**			**bhyām**			**bhis**		
Dat	**e**			**bhyām**			**bhyas**		
Abl	**as**			**bhyām**			**bhyas**		
Gen	**as**			**os**			**ām**		
Loc	**i**			**os**			**su**		
	Singular			Dual			Plural		

These endings are generally applied to most stems using **sandhi** rules. For example, the masculine nominative plural standard ending is **as**. When **as** is added to **nara**, the word for "men" becomes **narās**. These standard endings are listed by **Pāṇini** in a **sūtra** (4.1.2) that begins with **su** and ends with **p**. **Pāṇini** therefore calls the nominal endings **sup**.

2. On the following page is the declension for feminine nouns ending with **ā** in their stem form:

Stem: **mālā** (feminine) garland

	Singular	Dual	Plural
Nom	माला **mālā**	माले **māle**	मालास् **mālās**
Acc	मालाम् **mālām**	माले **māle**	मालास् **mālās**
Inst	मालया **mālayā**	मालाभ्याम् **mālābhyām**	मालाभिस् **mālābhis**
Dat	मालायै **mālāyai**	मालाभ्याम् **mālābhyām**	मालाभ्यस् **mālābhyas**
Abl	मालायास् **mālāyās**	मालाभ्याम् **mālābhyām**	मालाभ्यस् **mālābhyas**
Gen	मालायास् **mālāyās**	मालयोस् **mālayos**	मालानाम् **mālānām**
Loc	मालायाम् **mālāyām**	मालयोस् **mālayos**	मालासु **mālāsu**
Voc	माले **māle**	माले **māle**	मालास् **mālās**

3. Feminine nouns must have feminine adjectives. Masculine and neuter adjectives normally are declined like **nara** and **phala**. If the noun is feminine, the adjective is declined like **ā** or **ī** stems. (The feminine stem ending in **ī** will be studied in Lesson 13.) The dictionary will indicate how the feminine adjective is formed. For example:

kupita mf(**ā**)n **bhīta** mf(**ā**)n
dhārmika mf(**ī**)n **sundara** mf(**ī**)n

If the dictionary is unmarked (mfn), the adjective is formed with **ā**.

4. While the first and second person pronoun have only one declension, the third person pronoun has three declensions—one for each gender:
Stem: **tad** (masculine) he

		Singular	Dual	Plural
he, they	Nom	सस् **sas**	तौ **tau**	ते **te**
to him, them	Acc	तम् **tam**	तौ **tau**	तान् **tān**
with him, them	Inst	तेन **tena**	ताभ्याम् **tābhyām**	तैस् **tais**
for him, them	Dat	तस्मै **tasmai**	ताभ्याम् **tābhyām**	तेभ्यस् **tebhyas**
from him, them	Abl	तस्मात् **tasmāt**	ताभ्याम् **tābhyām**	तेभ्यस् **tebhyas**
his, their	Gen	तस्य **tasya**	तयोस् **tayos**	तेषाम् **teṣām**
on him, them	Loc	तस्मिन् **tasmin**	तयोस् **tayos**	तेषु **teṣu**

5. With **sandhi**, **sas**, the masculine nominative singular, drops the final **s** before all consonants and all vowels but **a**. It usually appears as **sa**. Only before **a** does it change to **so**. For example:

स गच्छति		सो ऽत्र	
sa gacchati	He goes.	**so 'tra**	He is here.

6. Here is the neuter third person pronoun:
Stem: **tad** (neuter) it

		Singular	Dual	Plural
it	Nom	तत् **tat**	ते **te**	तानि **tāni**
to it	Acc	तत् **tat**	ते **te**	तानि **tāni**
with it	Inst	तेन **tena**	ताभ्याम् **tābhyām**	तैस् **tais**
for it	Dat	तस्मै **tasmai**	ताभ्याम् **tābhyām**	तेभ्यस् **tebhyas**
from it	Abl	तस्मात् **tasmāt**	ताभ्याम् **tābhyām**	तेभ्यस् **tebhyas**
of it, its	Gen	तस्य **tasya**	तयोस् **tayos**	तेषाम् **teṣām**
on it	Loc	तस्मिन् **tasmin**	तयोस् **tayos**	तेषु **teṣu**

7. Notice that the nominative and accusative are the only forms in which the neuter differs from the masculine.

8. Here is the feminine third person pronoun:

Stem: **tad** (feminine) she

		Singular	Dual	Plural
she	Nom	सा **sā**	ते **te**	तास् **tās**
to her	Acc	ताम् **tām**	ते **te**	तास् **tās**
with her	Inst	तया **tayā**	ताभ्याम् **tābhyām**	ताभिस् **tābhis**
for her	Dat	तस्यै **tasyai**	ताभ्याम् **tābhyām**	ताभ्यस् **tābhyas**
from her	Abl	तस्यास् **tasyās**	ताभ्याम् **tābhyām**	ताभ्यस् **tābhyas**
her	Gen	तस्यास् **tasyās**	तयोस् **tayos**	तासाम् **tāsām**
on her	Loc	तस्याम् **tasyām**	तयोस् **tayos**	तासु **tāsu**

9. The third person pronoun can act as a pronoun or a demonstrative pronoun meaning "that." For example:

    स गच्छति ।
    sa gacchati
    He goes. ("He" is a pronoun.)

    स नरो गच्छति ।
    sa naro gacchati
    That man goes. ("That" is a demonstrative pronoun.)

10. The demonstrative pronoun goes in front of the noun it is used with and corresponds to the noun in case, gender, and number. For example:

    स बालो गच्छति ।
    sa bālo gacchati
    That boy goes.

    बालस्तं ग्रामं गच्छति ।
    bālas taṃ grāmaṃ gacchati
    The boy goes to that village.

    रामस्तस्मिन्नश्वे तिष्ठति ।
    rāmas tasminn aśve tiṣṭhati
    Rāma stands on that horse.
    (Note the **sandhi** change for **tasmin**. See page 126.)

VOCABULARY

SANSKRIT		ENGLISH
अविद्या	**avidyā** (fem)	ignorance
इव	**iva** (ind)	as if, like (used after verbs, nouns, or adjectives)
कथा	**kathā** (fem)	story
कन्या	**kanyā** (fem)	girl
कुपिता	**kupitā** (fem adj)	angry
छाया	**chāyā** (fem)	shadow
पुत्रिका	**putrikā** (fem)	daughter
प्रजा	**prajā** (fem)	child, subject (of a king)
बाला	**bālā** (fem)	girl
भार्या	**bhāryā** (fem)	wife
भीता	**bhītā** (fem adj)	afraid
माला	**mālā** (fem)	garland
विद्या	**vidyā** (fem)	knowledge
सीता	**sītā** (fem)	Sītā (wife of Rāma)
सेना	**senā** (fem)	army

EXERCISES

1. Write in **devanāgarī**, with correct **sandhi**, and translate. Use the vocabulary list and tables located in the back of the text.

a. **rāmena saha**

b. **śāstrāni**

c. **phale aśve staḥ**

d. **sas gacchati**

e. **sas bālas āgacchati**

f. **bālas mām āgacchati**

g. **sā bālā mām āgacchati**

h. **tām gacchati**

i. **sas bālas gacchati**

j. **sā bālā gacchati**

k. **sas bālas iva gacchāmi**

l. **aho rāma**

m. **tasmin vane sas vasati**

n. **sītāyās mālā**

2. Take out the **sandhi** and translate the following:

a. सा सेना नृपं जयति ।

b. राम इव बालो धार्मिको ऽस्ति ।

c. तव प्रजा कथां पठति ।

d. गजस्य च्छायायां प्रजास्तिष्ठन्ति ।

e. सीता नृपस्य पुत्रिकास्ति ।

f. स आचार्यस्य भार्यां सेवते ।

g. नृपस्य पुत्रिका ।

h. विद्यया शिष्यो ऽमृतं लभते ।

i. सा बालेव सीता गृहं गच्छति ।

3. Translate the following into Sanskrit, including **sandhi**, and then write in **devanāgarī**:

   a. There is a girl, Sītā by name, in that village.

   b. The daughter of the virtuous king is very afraid.

   c. "He tells me again," that subject says.

   d. "Aha! I remember that story!" the girl says.

   e. With knowledge, you obtain immortality; with ignorance, you obtain suffering.

f. Like those girls, Sītā reads books.

g. "Where is our daughter?" the hero asks his wife.

h. The wife of Rāma is Sītā.

i. The hero obtains a garland and thus obtains a wife.

j. "Without Sītā, I am as if without the sun," Rāma says.

THE MONKEY AND THE CROCODILE

4. Translate the following story. The vocabulary is given afterward:

a. अस्ति गङ्गायां कुम्भीरः ।

b. तस्य मित्रं वानरो गङ्गायास्तटे वसति ।

c. प्रतिदिनं वानरः पक्वानि फलानि निक्षिपति ।

d. कुम्भीरः फलानि खादति ।

e. वानरस्य हृदयं मिष्टमस्तीति कुम्भीरस्य भार्या वदति ।

f. भार्या हृदयं खादितुमिच्छति ।

g. अहो वानर मम गृहमागच्छेति कुम्भीरो वानरं वदति ।

h. एवमस्त्विति वानरो वदति ।

i. तस्य पृष्ठे कुम्भीरो वानरं वहति ।

j. गङ्गाया मध्ये कुम्भीरः सत्यं वदति ।

k. मम हृदयं वृक्षे भवतीति वानरो भाषते ।

l. पुनर्मां तत्र नयसीति वानरो भाषते ।

m. कुम्भीरो वानरं गङ्गायास्तटे नयति ।

n. वानरो वृक्षमुच्छलति ।

o. वानरो वृक्षस्य बिले पश्यति ।

p. कश्चिन्मम हृदयं चोरयति स्मेति वानरो वदति ।

q. एवं कुम्भीरो वानरश्च मित्रे तिष्ठतः ।

VOCABULARY

a. **gaṅgā** (fem, **ā** declension) Ganges
kumbhīra (mas) crocodile

b. **mitram** (neuter) friend
vānara (mas) monkey. Appears first as an appositional (his friend, a monkey)
taṭa (mas) bank (of the river)

c. **pratidinam** (ind) everyday
pakva mf(**ā**)n (adj) ripe
nikṣipati (3rd per sing) throws down

d. **khādati** (3rd per sing) eats

e. **hṛdayam** (n) heart
miṣṭa mf(**ā**)n (adj) sweet
bhāryā (fem, **ā** declension) wife

f. **khāditum** (infinitive—treated like an accusative) to eat
icchati (3rd per sing) wants (**khāditum icchati** = wants to eat)

g. **āgaccha** (2nd per sing imperative)

h. **evam astu** (ind) O.K., so let it be

i. **pṛṣṭham** (n) back
vahati (3rd per sing) he carries

j. **madhyam** (n) middle

k. **vṛkṣa** (mas) tree

l. **nayati** (3rd per sing) he takes

n. **ucchalati** (3rd per sing) he jumps up

o. **bilam** (n) hole

p. **kaś cit** (ind) someone
corayati (3rd per sing) he steals
sma (ind) makes verb before it in past tense

q. **tiṣṭhati** (3rd per sing) remains

12

LESSON TWELVE

Alphabet: Numerals; cardinal and ordinal numbers

Grammar: Nouns in **i** and the gerund

Vocabulary: Nouns in **i**

ALPHABET: NUMBERS

1. Here are the numerals (**saṃkhyā**) and cardinal numbers from one to ten. Alternate forms for some numerals are given in parentheses.

NUMERALS		CARDINAL NUMBERS	
Arabic	**devanāgarī**	English	Sanskrit
1.	१ (१)	one	**eka**
2.	२	two	**dvi**
3.	३	three	**tri**
4.	४	four	**catur**
5.	५ (५)	five	**pañca**
6.	६	six	**ṣaṣ**
7.	७	seven	**sapta**
8.	८ (८)	eight	**aṣṭa**
9.	९ (९)	nine	**nava**
10.	१०	ten	**daśa**

2. The **devanāgarī** numerals combine just like Arabic numerals (since Arabic numerals were formed from Sanskrit). For example:

11	११
12	१२

3. The numerals (१, २, ३, etc) will be written at the end of each sentence in the exercises. For now, we will not use the cardinal numbers (**eka**, **dvi**, etc.) as part of the sentences, since their declension is complex.

4. Here are the ordinal numbers:

First	**prathama**	Sixth	**ṣaṣṭha**
Second	**dvitīya**	Seventh	**saptama**
Third	**tṛtīya**	Eighth	**aṣṭama**
Fourth	**caturtha** (or **turīya**)	Ninth	**navama**
Fifth	**pañcama**	Tenth	**daśama**

5. The ordinal numbers will be used in the exercises, because their declensions are easier than the cardinal numbers. The ordinal numbers are used like adjectives, going before the noun they modify and agreeing with it in gender and case. The number will be singular.

6. The ordinal numbers follow the short **a** declension for the masculine and neuter. Here are the feminine stems. (The feminine **ī** will be learned in Lesson 13.)

First	**prathamā**	Sixth	**ṣaṣṭhī**
Second	**dvitīyā**	Seventh	**saptamī**
Third	**tṛtīyā**	Eighth	**aṣṭamī**
Fourth	**caturthī** (or **turīyā**)	Ninth	**navamī**
Fifth	**pañcamī**	Tenth	**daśamī**

Compare the **devanāgarī** numerals with other scripts:

COMPARATIVE TABLE OF NUMERALS

	1	2	3	4	5	6	7	8	9	0
Hieratic	[illegible]	[illegible]	[illegible]	[illegible]	[illegible]	[illegible]	[illegible]	[illegible]	[illegible]	
Gupta	𑁒	𑁓	𑁔	𑁕	𑁖	𑁗	𑁘	𑁙	𑁚	
Maledive	[illegible]	[illegible]	[illegible]	[illegible]	[illegible]	[illegible]	[illegible]	[illegible]	[illegible]	
Lepcha	᱁	᱂	᱃	᱄	᱅	᱆	᱇	᱈	᱉	᱀
Tibetan	༡	༢	༣	༤	༥	༦	༧	༨	༩	༠
Nepali	१	२	३	४	५	६	७	८	९	०
Devanāgarī	१	२	३	४	५	६	७	८	९	०
Kashmiri	𑇑	𑇒	𑇓	𑇔	𑇕	𑇖	𑇗	𑇘	𑇙	𑇐
Bengali	১	২	৩	৪	৫	৬	৭	৮	৯	০
Assamese	১	২	৩	৪	৫	৬	৭	৮	৯	০
Telugu	౧	౨	౩	౪	౫	౬	౭	౮	౯	౦
Tamil	௧	௨	௩	௪	௫	௬	௭	௮	௯	௰
Malabar	൧	൨	൩	൪	൫	൬	൭	൮	൯	൦
Sinhalese	𑇡	𑇢	𑇣	𑇤	𑇥	𑇦	𑇧	𑇨	𑇩	𑇪
Burmese	၁	၂	၃	၄	၅	၆	၇	၈	၉	၀
Siamese	๑	๒	๓	๔	๕	๖	๗	๘	๙	๐
Cambodian	១	២	៣	៤	៥	៦	៧	៨	៩	០
" (simplified)	[illegible]	[illegible]	[illegible]	[illegible]	[illegible]	[illegible]	[illegible]	[illegible]	[illegible]	[illegible]
Javanese	꧑	꧒	꧓	꧔	꧕	꧖	꧗	꧘	꧙	꧐

7. Compare the cardinal numbers with numbers from several Romance languages:

English	Sanskrit	Italian	French	Spanish
one	**eka**	uno	un	uno
two	**dvi**	due	deux	dos
three	**tri**	tre	trois	tres
four	**catur**	quattro	quatre	cuatro
five	**pañca**	cinque	cinq	cinco
six	**ṣaṣ**	sei	six	seis
seven	**sapta**	sette	sept	siete
eight	**aṣṭa**	otto	huit	ocho
nine	**nava**	nove	neuf	nueve
ten	**daśa**	dieci	dix	diez

GRAMMAR: NOUNS IN I, THE GERUND

1. Here are the masculine and feminine declensions for **i** nouns. They differ in only two forms (the accusative plural and the instrumental singular).

Stem: **agni** (masculine) fire; **kīrti** (feminine) glory

Nom	अग्निस् **agnis**	अग्नी **agnī**	अग्नयस् **agnayas**
Acc	अग्निम् **agnim**	अग्नी **agnī**	अग्नीन् कीर्तीस् **agnīn / kīrtīs**
Inst	अग्निना कीर्त्या **agninā / kīrtyā**	अग्निभ्याम् **agnibhyām**	अग्निभिस् **agnibhis**
Dat	अग्नये कीर्त्यै **agnaye (kīrtyai)**	अग्निभ्याम् **agnibhyām**	अग्निभ्यस् **agnibhyas**
Abl	अग्नेस् कीर्त्यास् **agnes (kīrtyās)**	अग्निभ्याम् **agnibhyām**	अग्निभ्यस् **agnibhyas**
Gen	अग्नेस् कीर्त्यास् **agnes (kīrtyās)**	अग्न्योस् **agnyos**	अग्नीनाम् **agnīnām**
Loc	अग्नौ कीर्त्याम् **agnau (kīrtyām)**	अग्न्योस् **agnyos**	अग्निषु **agniṣu**
Voc	अग्ने **agne**	अग्नी **agnī**	अग्नयस् **agnayas**

2. The singular dative, ablative, genitive, and locative have an optional feminine form. For example, the feminine dative singular is **kīrtaye** or **kīrtyai**. The feminine instrumental singular is **kīrtyā**.

3. Now we will study the gerund, which is a participle formed from a verb. The gerund indicates prior action. The sentence, "Rāma speaks and goes," could be formed with a gerund. It would be: "Having spoken, Rāma goes." "Having spoken" is the gerund.

> **uditvā rāmo gacchati**
> Having spoken, Rāma goes.
> (gerund)

4. Because the gerund continues the action, it is sometimes called a continuative or conjunctive participle.

5. The gerund is used with only one subject.

6. The gerund has the meaning of doing something first, whether the main verb is past, present, or future. A series of gerunds may be used, but they must always be followed by a main verb. Each gerund follows in time the one before it, and the main verb comes last in time, as well as position in the sentence. For example:

> **gajaṃ dṛṣṭvā jalaṃ labdhvā rāmo gacchati**
> Having seen the elephant, having obtained water, Rāma goes.

7. There are several alternative translations:

> Seeing the elephant, obtaining water, Rāma goes.
> After seeing the elephant and after obtaining water, Rāma goes.
> After having seen the elephant and after having obtained water, Rāma goes.

8. Everything that goes with the gerund, such as the accusative, is usually placed before it.

9. The gerund is easy to recognize because it is not declined at all. It is sometimes called the absolutive, because it stays in the same form. It is usually formed from the root by adding **-tvā** to the end (**ktvā**). If there is a prefix, **-ya** is added at the end (**lyap**).

10. Here are the forms for the gerund (√**as** has no gerund):

VERBS PRIMARILY TAKING ACTIVE ENDINGS

Root	3rd Per Sing	Gerund	
ā + √**gam**	**āgacchati**	**āgamya** (also **āgatya**)	having come
√**gam**	**gacchati -te**	**gatvā**	having gone
√**cint**	**cintayati -te**	**cintayitvā**	having thought
√**ji**	**jayati -te**	**jitvā**	having conquered
√**dṛś** (**paś**)	**paśyati -te**	**dṛṣṭvā**	having seen
√**paṭh**	**paṭhati -te**	**paṭhitvā**	having read
√**prach**	**pṛcchati -te**	**pṛṣṭvā**	having asked
√**bhū**	**bhavati -te**	**bhūtvā**	having been
√**vad**	**vadati -te**	**uditvā**	having said
√**vas**	**vasati -te**	**uṣitvā**	having lived
√**sthā**	**tiṣṭhati -te**	**sthitvā**	having stood
√**smṛ**	**smarati -te**	**smṛtvā**	having remembered

VERBS PRIMARILY TAKING MIDDLE ENDINGS

√**bhāṣ**	**bhāṣate -ti**	**bhāṣitvā**	having said
√**man**	**manyate -ti**	**matvā**	having thought
√**labh**	**labhate -ti**	**labdhvā**	having obtained
√**sev**	**sevate -ti**	**sevitvā**	having served

VOCABULARY

SANSKRIT		ENGLISH
अग्नि	**agni** (mas)	fire
अतिथि	**atithi** (mas)	guest
ऋषि	**ṛṣi** (mas)	seer, sage
कवि	**kavi** (mas)	poet
कीर्ति	**kīrti** (fem)	glory, fame
भूमि	**bhūmi** (fem)	earth
शान्ति	**śānti** (fem)	peace
सिद्ध	**siddha** (mas), **siddhā** (fem)	one who attains perfection
सिद्धि	**siddhi** (fem)	perfection, attainment, proof

EXERCISES

1. Translate the following sentences. Use the vocabulary and tables listed at the end of the text.

a. अग्निं दृष्ट्वा गृहादश्वो गच्छति ।१।

b. शिष्यो ग्रामे वसति ।२।

c. ऋषयः शास्त्राणां सूक्तानि पश्यन्ति ।३।

d. नृपो दशममतिथिं सेवते ।४।

e. ग्रामं जित्वा वीरः कीर्तिं लभते ।५।

f. सिद्धो ग्रामे वसति ।६।

g. अहो राम कुत्र गच्छसीति द्वितीयो वीरः पृच्छति ।७।

h. पुस्तकं पठित्वा कविस्तच्चिन्तयति ।८।

i. सत्येन सह शान्तिरागच्छति ।९।

j. भूमौ वसाम इति प्रजा वदन्ति ।१०।

2. Write the following sentences in Sanskrit:

a. After conquering the army, the hero obtains fame on earth.

b. Like Sītā and Rāma, the student goes to the forest.

c. After serving her third guest, Sītā speaks to Rāma.

d. In the story, Rāma obtains fame.

e. The hero does not conquer ignorance.

f. The king, Rāma by name, is very virtuous.

g. "How do you obtain perfection?" the second student asks.

h. Having lived in the forest with his wife, the king, Rāma by name, goes to the village.

i. Having obtained peace, perfection, and glory, the seer goes to the beautiful forest.

j. Thus having seen his wife on the elephant, the hero goes to her.

13

LESSON THIRTEEN

Alphabet:	The **sandhi** rules for combining vowels
Grammar:	Feminine nouns in **ī** Relative-correlative clauses
Vocabulary:	Nouns in **ī** Relative and correlative adverbs

ALPHABET: VOWEL SANDHI

1. The following chart shows the changes that vowels often undergo. These changes are called **guṇa** and **vṛddhi** changes:

	guṇa	vṛddhi	Corresponding Semi-vowel
a	**a**	**ā**	
ā	**ā**	**ā**	
i, ī	**e**	**ai**	**y**
ṛ	**ar**	**ār**	**r**
ḷ	**al**	**āl**	**l**
u, ū	**o**	**au**	**v**

2. This important chart will help you understand how vowels combine in both internal and external **sandhi**. Later on, it will help you understand how roots are strengthened (by **guṇa** or **vṛddhi**) to form verbs and nominals. For example:

Root	guṇa	vṛddhi
√vid	**veda**	**vaidya**
√div	**deva**	**daivika**

3. Memorize the above chart and then memorize the **sandhi** rules for combining vowels that follow:

4. SIMILAR VOWELS

ă + ă = ā

राम + अश्वस् = रामाश्वः

rāma + aśvas = rāmāśvaḥ

ĭ + ĭ = ī

गच्छति + इति = गच्छतीति

gacchati + iti = gacchatīti

ŭ + ŭ = ū

गुरु + उप = गुरूप

guru + upa = gurūpa

ṛ + ṛ = ṝ

पितृ + ऋषि = पितॄषि

pitṛ + ṛṣi = pitṝṣi

These rules apply first. Then the following rules apply.

5. DISSIMILAR VOWELS

ĭ + vowel = **y**vowel ("vowel" means any short or long vowel)

गच्छति + अश्वम् =

गच्छत्यश्वम्

gacchati + aśvam =

gacchaty aśvam

ŭ + vowel = **v**vowel

गुरु + अश्वम् = गुर्वश्वम्

guru + aśvam = gurv aśvam

ṛ + vowel = **r**vowel

पितृ + अत्र = पित्रत्र

pitṛ + atra = pitr atra

6. **e + a = e '** — **ग्रामे + अत्र = ग्रामे ऽत्र**
grāme + atra = grāme 'tra

e + vowel = **a** vowel — **ग्रामे + इति = ग्राम इति**
grāme + iti = grāma iti

7. **ai** + vowel = **ā** vowel — **तस्मै + अत्र = तस्मा अत्र**
tasmai + atra = tasmā atra

An **o** seldom occurs in a final position before **sandhi** is applied.

au + vowel = **āv**vowel — **गजौ + इति = गजाविति**
gajau + iti = gajāv iti

8. FINAL **ă** PLUS A DISSIMILAR VOWEL

ă + ĭ = e — **तत्र + इत = तत्रेति**
tatra + iti = tatreti

ă + ŭ = o — **कठ + उपनिषद् = कठोपनिषद्**
kaṭha + upaniṣad = kaṭhopaniṣad

ă + ṛ = ar — **सत्य + ऋतम् = सत्यर्तम्**
satya + ṛtam = satya rtam

ă + e, ai = ai	तत्र + एव = तत्रैव **tatra + eva = tatraiva**
ă + o, au = au	अत्र + ओकस् = अत्रौकः **atra + okas = atraukaḥ**

9. Some vowels (**pragṛhya**) are not subject to **sandhi**. They are:

   a. the letters **ī**, **ū**, and **e**, when they serve as dual endings. For example, **bāle āgacchataḥ** (The two girls come.) needs no **sandhi**.

   b. the final vowel of an interjection. For example, **aho aśva** (Oh horse!) needs no **sandhi**.

GRAMMAR: NOUNS IN Ī, RELATIVE-CORRELATIVES

1. Here is the declension for feminine nouns ending with ī in their stem form:

Stem: **vāpī** (feminine) pond

	Singular	Dual	Plural
Nom	वापी vāpī	वाप्यौ vāpyau	वाप्यस् vāpyas
Acc	वापीम् vāpīm	वाप्यौ vāpyau	वापीस् vāpīs
Inst	वाप्या vāpyā	वापीभ्याम् vāpībhyām	वापीभिस् vāpībhis
Dat	वाप्यै vāpyai	वापीभ्याम् vāpībhyām	वापीभ्यस् vāpībhyas
Abl	वाप्यास् vāpyās	वापीभ्याम् vāpībhyām	वापीभ्यस् vāpībhyas
Gen	वाप्यास् vāpyās	वाप्योस् vāpyos	वापीनाम् vāpīnām
Loc	वाप्याम् vāpyām	वाप्योस् vāpyos	वापीषु vāpīṣu
Voc	वापि vāpi	वाप्यौ vāpyau	वाप्यस् vāpyas

2. Now we will learn about relative and correlative clauses. In English, the sentence "I see where the king lives," contains two separate clauses: "I see" and "where the king lives." The sentence contains a subordinate, or relative clause ("where the king lives"), and an independent or correlative clause ("I see"). For example:

I see where the king lives.

correlative relative

3. In Sanskrit, the relative clause usually goes first and the correlative goes second. The relative clause is introduced by a relative adverb (indeclinable) and the correlative clause by a correlative adverb.

Where the king lives, there I see.

relative clause correlative clause

Where the king lives, there I see.

relative adverb correlative adverb

yatra nṛpo vasati tatra ahaṃ paśyāmi

relative clause correlative clause

yatra nṛpo vasati tatra ahaṃ paśyāmi

relative adverb correlative adverb

4. Here are the relative adverbs and their correlative partners (none are declined):

yataḥ	since	**tataḥ**	therefore
yatra	where	**tatra**	there
yathā	since, as	**tathā**	so, therefore
yadā	when	**tadā**	then
yadi	if	**tadā**	then

5. Here are some examples:

When he goes, then I remember.
yadā gacchati tadā smarāmi

I go if you go. (becomes)
If you go, then I go.
yadi gacchasi tadā gacchāmi

You obtain fruit where the forest is. (becomes)
Where the forest is, there you obtain fruit.
yatra vanam asti tatra phalāni labhase

6. There is also a relative-correlative pronoun, **yad** and **tad** ("who" and "he"). This construction would be used to translate this sentence:

The man who goes is the king.

|________|

relative clause

7. In Sanskrit, the relative clause contains the relative pronoun **yad**, and the correlative clause contains the correlative pronoun **tad**. Sometimes the correlative pronoun may be omitted. The pronoun **yad** follows the declension of **tad** (mas, n, fem):

who man goes, he is the king
|____________| |___________|
relative clause correlative clause

yo naro gacchati sa nṛpo 'sti
|______________| |___________|
relative clause correlative clause

8. Both "who" (**yo**) and "he" (**sa**) refer back to the man, who is called the antecedent. In English, the antecedent goes directly before the relative pronoun (who). In Sanskrit, the antecedent usually follows the relative pronoun (who) or the correlative pronoun (he):

who man goes, he is the king
yo naro gacchati sa nṛpo 'sti
|_____|
antecedent

or

who goes, that man is the king
yo gacchati sa naro nṛpo 'sti
|_____|
antecedent

9. The relative and correlative pronouns take the gender and number of the antecedent. The case of the antecedent depends upon its role in each clause. Study the following examples:

I see the man who is going. (becomes)
which man is going, him I see
yo naro gacchati taṃ paśyāmi

|____|
antecedent

|_________________| |____________|
relative clause correlative clause

or

who is going, that man I see
yo gacchati taṃ naraṃ paśyāmi

|_____|
antecedent

|_________| |___________________|
relative clause correlative clause

The king sees the elephant on which I stand. (becomes)
on which elephant I stand, him the king sees
yasmin gaje tiṣṭhāmi taṃ nṛpaḥ paśyati

|_____|
antecedent

|____________________| |________________|
relative clause correlative clause

or

on which I stand, that elephant the king sees

yasmiṃs tiṣṭhāmi taṃ gajaṃ nṛpaḥ paśyati

|______|

antecedent

|____________________|| |___________________________|

relative clause correlative clause

10. Notice that the relative pronoun (**yad**) and the correlative pronoun (**tad**) agree with each other in gender and number, but may differ in case. Like the antecedent, the relative word and the correlative word take a case that is determined by their role in the clause. The nominative masculine singular, **yas**, follows normal **sandhi** rules. Study the following examples:

I see the man with whom Rāma goes.
(becomes)
with which man Rāma goes, him I see

येन नरेण सह रामो गच्छति तमहं पश्यामि ।

yena nareṇa saha rāmo gacchati tam ahaṃ paśyāmi

or

with whom Rāma goes, that man I see

येन रामो गच्छति तं नरमहं पश्यामि ।

yena rāmo gacchati taṃ naram ahaṃ paśyāmi

Rāma lives in the village from which I am coming.
(becomes)
from which village I am coming, in it Rāma lives

यस्माद्ग्रामादागच्छामि तस्मिन्रामो वसति ।

yasmād grāmād āgacchāmi tasmin rāmo vasati

or

from which I am coming in that village Rāma lives

यस्मादागच्छामि तस्मिन्ग्रामे रामो वसति ।

yasmād āgacchāmi tasmin grāme rāmo vasati

VOCABULARY

SANSKRIT		ENGLISH
धार्मिकी	**dhārmikī** (fem, adj)	virtuous
नदी	**nadī** (fem)	river
पत्नी	**patnī** (fem)	wife
मित्रम्	**mitram** (neuter)	friend
यद्	**yad** (pronoun)	who, what, which (declined the same as **tad**)
वापी	**vāpī** (fem)	pond
सुन्दरी	**sundarī** (fem, adj)	beautiful

SANSKRIT (relative adverbs)		ENGLISH	SANSKRIT (correlative adverbs)		ENGLISH
यतः	**yataḥ**	since	ततः	**tataḥ**	therefore
यत्र	**yatra**	where	तत्र	**tatra**	there
यथा	**yathā**	since, as	तथा	**tathā**	so, therefore
यदा	**yadā**	when	तदा	**tadā**	then
यदि	**yadi**	if	तदा	**tadā**	then

EXERCISES

1. Translate the following:

 a. यत्र शान्तिस्तत्र सिद्धिः ।१।

 b. या मम पत्न्याः पुत्रिकास्ति सा बालात्र वसति ।२।

 c. सीता सुन्दरी नृपस्य पुत्रिकास्तीति रामो वदति ।३।

 d. यथाश्वा अत्र नागच्छन्ति तथा नरा बालाश्च तत्र गच्छन्ति ।४।

 e. नदीं गत्वा मित्रे पुस्तकानि पठतः ।५।

 f. यदा सेना नृपं सेवते तदा धार्मिको नृपो जयति ।६।

 g. यदि नरः सिद्धिं लभते तदा स ऋषिर्भवते ।७।

 h. यस्तस्यातिथिर्भवति तस्मै बालाय कविः कथां पठति ।८।

i. नरो मित्रेण सह सुन्दरीं नदीं गच्छति ।९।

j. यस्मादहमागच्छामि तं ग्रामं वीरः स्मरति ।१०।

2. Translate the following into Sanskrit:

a. The boy obtains water from the river.

b. The wife sees the fruit which is in the pond.

c. Having obtained a garland, our guest goes to the village.

d. He lives like a king when his wife serves him.

e. Sītā, who is the wife of Rāma, obtains fame on earth.

f. The virtuous king sees the boy who is coming.

g. The student, having thought, asks the poet about the river.

h. That beautiful wife lives without suffering.

i. Ignorance is like a shadow for the man who sees.

j. When the daughter of the king comes, then the subjects stand.

14

LESSON FOURTEEN

Alphabet: The **sandhi** rules for final **s**

Grammar: Verb prefixes and the imperfect active

Vocabulary: More verbs

ALPHABET: SANDHI RULES FOR FINAL S

Now we will memorize the **sandhi** rules for words ending in **s**. These rules were presented in charts in Lesson 9. Both charts in Lesson 9 present the same rules, but it will be easier to follow the structure of the second chart on page 111. While the first word ends in **s**, the second word may begin with any letter of the alphabet. Notice that the chart breaks the alphabet into three parts. The chart is arranged according to which section of the alphabet the second word begins. Here is one way of dividing the alphabet in order to learn these rules:

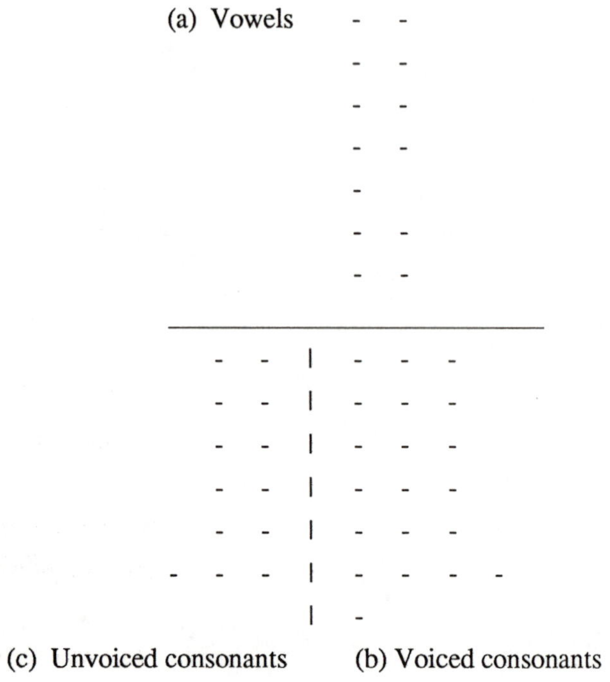

```
                    (a) Vowels   -  -
                                 -  -
                                 -  -
                                 -  -
                                 -
                                 -  -
                                 -  -
                  ________________________
                     -  -  |  -  -  -
                     -  -  |  -  -  -
                     -  -  |  -  -  -
                     -  -  |  -  -  -
                     -  -  |  -  -  -
                  -  -  -  |  -  -  -  -
                           |  -
(c) Unvoiced consonants       (b) Voiced consonants
```

(a) If the second word begins in a vowel, there are four rules:

Second word begins in any of the following:

a	**ā**
i	**ī**
u	**ū**
ṛ	**ṝ**
ḷ	
e	**ai**
o	**au**

(1) If the first word ends in **as** and the second begins in **a**, the **as** changes to **o**, and the **a** is deleted (marked by an apostrophe in roman script or **avagraha** in **devanāgarī**). For example:

as + a = o '

रामस् + अत्र = रामो ऽत्र

rāmas + atra = rāmo 'tra

(2) If the first word ends in **as** and the second word begins in any vowel (except **a**), the **as** changes to **a**:

as + vowel = **a** vowel

रामस् + आगच्छति = राम आगच्छति

rāmas + āgacchati = rāma āgacchati

(3) If the first word ends in **ās** and the second word begins in any vowel, the **ās** changes to **ā**:

ās + vowel = **ā** + vowel

नरास् + **इति** = **नरा इति**

narās + iti = narā iti

(4) If the first word ends in any other vowel before the final **s**, and the second word begins in a vowel, then the **s** changes to an **r**. For example:

os + vowel = **or**vowel

नद्योस् + **अत्र** = **नद्योरत्र**

nadyos + atra = nadyor atra

(b) If the second word begins in a voiced consonant, there are three rules:

Second word begins in :

ga	**gha**	**ṅa**	
ja	**jha**	**ña**	
ḍa	**ḍha**	**ṇa**	
da	**dha**	**na**	
ba	**bha**	**ma**	
ya	**ra**	**la**	**va**
ha			

(1) If the first word ends in **as**, it becomes **o**:

as + voiced consonant = **o** voiced consonant

रामस् + गच्छति = रामो गच्छति

rāmas + gacchati = rāmo gacchati

(2) If the first word ends in **ās**, it becomes **ā**:

ās + voiced consonant = **ā** voiced consonant

नरास् + गच्छन्ति = नरा गच्छन्ति

narās + gacchanti = narā gacchanti

(3) If the first word ends in any other vowel before the final **s**, the **s** becomes **r** (unless the second word begins with an **r**). For example:

os + voiced consonant = **or**voiced consonant

नरयोस् + गच्छति = नरयोर्गच्छति

narayos + gacchati = narayor gacchati

A double **r** does not occur. If the second word begins in **r**, the first **r** is dropped and the preceding vowel made long, if it is short.

Note that the last two rules (2 and 3) are the same as the rules (3 and 4) for second words beginning in a vowel.

(c) For the third group, the second word begins in an unvoiced consonant. For this group, the rules are the same when the first word ends in **as**, **ās**, or any other vowel before the **s**. There are four rules:

Second word begins in:

ka	**kha**		
ca	**cha**		
ṭa	**ṭha**		
ta	**tha**		
pa	**pha**		
śa	**ṣa**	**sa**	end of line

(1) If the second word begins in **ca** or **cha**, the **s** (with any vowel preceding it) changes to **ś**. For example:

as + ca = aśca

रामस् + च = रामश्च

rāmas + ca = rāmaś ca

(2) If the second word begins in **ṭa** or **ṭha**, the **s** changes to **ṣ**:

as + ṭ = aṣṭ

रामस् + टीका = रामष्टीका

rāmas + ṭīkā = rāmaṣ ṭīkā

(3) If the second word begins in **ta** or **tha**, the **s** stays an **s**. This is the only case where the **s** remains unchanged:

as + ta = asta

रामस् + तत्र = रामस्तत्र

rāmas + tatra = rāmas tatra

The above three rules might best be learned visually, using the **devanāgarī** script. In each case the **s** becomes the sibilant that corresponds with the following letter, whether palatal (**ca**, **cha**), retroflex (**ṭa**, **ṭha**), or dental (**ta**, **tha**).

(4) All other unvoiced consonants (**ka**, **kha**, **pa**, **pha**, **śa**, **ṣa**, and **sa**) cause the **s** to become ḥ. The end of the line also causes the **s** to become ḥ. For example:

as + k = aḥ k

रामस् + कुत्र = रामः कुत्र

rāmas + kutra = rāmaḥ kutra

GRAMMAR: PREFIXES, IMPERFECT ACTIVE VERBS

1. Verb prefixes (**upasarga**) are placed before verbs to modify the basic meaning of the verb. They are used much like verb prefixes in English, such as "remake" and "undo." We have already learned one prefix, **ā**, which changes "he goes" (**gacchati**) to "he comes" (**āgacchati**).

2. Here are two additional prefixes:

upa	towards, near
upagacchati	he goes toward, he approaches
prati	back to, against
pratigacchati	he goes back to, he returns.

3. The imperfect (**laṅ**) indicates past action. It is formed by putting an augment (**āgama**), **a**, before the present stem and using slightly different endings, the imperfect endings. For example:

a + **gaccha** + **t** becomes **agacchat** he went
a + **vada** + **t** becomes **avadat** he spoke

augment — stem — ending — imperfect

4. Here is the formation for the imperfect:

	Singular	Dual	Plural
3rd	अगच्छत् **agacchat**	अगच्छताम् **agacchatām**	अगच्छन् **agacchan**
2nd	अगच्छस् **agacchas**	अगच्छतम् **agacchatam**	अगच्छत **agacchata**
1st	अगच्छम् **agaccham**	अगच्छाव **agacchāva**	अगच्छाम **agacchāma**

5. Here are the endings for the present indicative that we have already learned. Notice that the imperfect has similar endings, but shorter:

	Singular	Dual	Plural
3rd	गच्छति **gacchati**	गच्छतः **gacchataḥ**	गच्छन्ति **gacchanti**
2nd	गच्छसि **gacchasi**	गच्छथः **gacchathaḥ**	गच्छथ **gacchatha**
1st	गच्छामि **gacchāmi**	गच्छावः **gacchāvaḥ**	गच्छामः **gacchāmaḥ**

6. The imperfect puts the augment, **a**, after the prefix but before the stem. The **sandhi** rules apply here. Study these examples:

प्रति	+ अ	+ गच्छ	+	त्	=	प्रत्यगच्छत्
prati	+ **a**	+ **gaccha**	+	**t**	=	**pratyagacchat**
						he returned
prefix	augment	stem		ending		imperfect

उप + अ + गच्छ + त् = उपागच्छत्

upa + a + gaccha + t = **upāgacchat**

he approached

आ + अ + गच्छ - अ+ अम् = आगच्छम्

ā + a + gaccha - a + am = **āgaccham**

I came

7. Often a verb that may take both active and middle endings will not do so with a prefix. The dictionary would then list the verb like this: **upa √gam upagacchati** (without -**te**).

VOCABULARY

SANSKRIT		ENGLISH
आ + नी	आनयति	
ā + √nī (active)	**ānayati**	he brings
उप + गम्	उपगच्छति	
upa + √gam (active)	**upagacchati**	he goes toward, he approaches
गुप्	गोपयति	
√gup (active)	**gopayati -te**	he protects
नी	नयति	
√nī (active)	**nayati -te**	he leads
पा	पिबति	
√pā (active)	**pibati -te**	he drinks
प्रति + गम्	प्रतिगच्छति	
prati + √gam (active)	**pratigacchati**	he goes back, he returns
बुध्	बोधति	
√budh (active)	**bodhati -te**	he knows
हस्	हसति	
√has (active)	**hasati -te**	he laughs

The gerund forms for each of these verbs is listed in the back of the text (pages 312-314). Remember that if a verb has a prefix, it forms a gerund with **-ya** rather than **-tvā**.

EXERCISES

1. Memorize the **sandhi** rules that take place when the first word ends in **s**.

2. Memorize the endings for the imperfect active.

3. Translate the following sentences into English:

a. यदा शिष्यो जलमानयति तदाचार्यस्तत्पिबति ।१।

b. बालो वापीं गजाननयत् ।२।

c. यो नरो ग्राममुपगच्छति तं कविर्वदति ।३।

d. वीरः कुपितान्नृपाद्ग्रामं गोपयतीति रामो ऽवदत् ।४।

e. वाप्यां गजं दृष्ट्वर्षिरहसदहसच्च ।५।

f. सुन्दरीं तव पत्नीं बोधामीति कन्या वीरमवदत् ।६।

g. यस्मिन्गृहे पत्न्यवसत्तत्सा प्रत्यगच्छत् ।७।

h. ऋषिः शान्तिं सत्यं सिद्धिममृतं सुखं च बोधति ।८।

i. वीरः सेनाया ग्राममगोपयत् ।९।

j. सुन्दरं नृपं दृष्ट्वा बालो ऽहसत् ।१०।

4. Translate the following into Sanskrit:

   a. The poet read the book as if he were drinking water.

   b. The hero asked, "How do I protect the village from the army?"

   c. How did sages live without fire?

   d. If the horses go back to river, then the boy leads them to the forest. (Use double accusative.)

   e. When a man does not know suffering, then he approaches perfection.

   f. The king, named Rāma, brought his wife, Sītā, a garland.

   g. By means of knowledge, a man conquers ignorance.

   h. The child drank the water which came from the river.

i. Having seen the river, the girl returned to her house.

j. The boy led the horses from the forest to the river. (double accusative)

15

LESSON FIFTEEN

Alphabet: The **sandhi** rules for final **m**

Grammar: More verb prefixes and the imperfect middle

Vocabulary: More verbs

ALPHABET: SANDHI RULES FOR FINAL M

1. If the first word ends in **m**, there are only two rules:

(a) If the next word begins in a consonant, the **m** becomes **ṃ** and is pronounced (and could be written) as the nasal corresponding to the first letter of the next word. For example:

पुत्रम् + गच्छामि = पुत्रं गच्छामि
putram + gacchāmi = putraṃ gacchāmi

(b) If the next word begins in a vowel or is at the end of a line, the **m** remains the same. The **m** remains the same because the mouth is not preparing to close at a specific point of contact as it would if the next word began with a consonant.
For example:

पुत्रम् + आगच्छामि = पुत्रमागच्छामि
putram + āgcchāmi = putram āgacchāmi

GRAMMAR:
VERB PREFIXES,
IMPERFECT MIDDLE

1. Here are two more verb prefixes. Some prefixes hardly change the meaning of the original stem, while others change the meaning so much that the new verb seems unrelated to its parts:

ud	up, up out
uttiṣṭhati	he stands up

(A **sandhi** rule changes the **d** to a **t**.)

udbhavati	he is born
ava	down, away, off
avagacchati	he understands

2. Here is a list of the major prefixes. It is not necessary to memorize this list. Just become familiar with the list so you will recognize a verb prefix in the future:

अति	**ati**	across, beyond, surpassing
अधि	**adhi**	above, over, on
अनु	**anu**	after, following
अन्तर्	**antar**	within, between
अप	**apa**	away, off
अपि	**api**	on, close on
अभि	**abhi**	to, against
अव	**ava**	down, away, off

आ	ā	back, return
उद्	ud	up, up out
उप	upa	towards
नि	ni	down, into
निस्	nis	out, forth
परा	parā	away, forth
परि	pari	around, about
प्र	pra	forward, onward, forth
प्रति	prati	back to, in reverse direction
वि	vi	apart, away, out
सम्	sam	together

3. Here is the imperfect middle, which is also used as a simple past tense:

Stem: **bhāṣ** (middle) speak

	Singular	Dual	Plural
3rd	अभाषत abhāṣata	अभाषेताम् abhāṣetām	अभाषन्त abhāṣanta
2nd	अभाषथाः abhāṣathāḥ	अभाषेथाम् abhāṣethām	अभाषध्वम् abhāṣadhvam
1st	अभाषे abhāṣe	अभाषावहि abhāṣāvahi	अभाषामहि abhāṣāmahi

4. Compare the imperfect endings with the present indicative endings:

	Singular	Dual	Plural
3rd	भाषते bhāṣate	भाषेते bhāṣete	भाषन्ते bhāṣante
2nd	भाषसे bhāṣase	भाषेथे bhāṣethe	भाषध्वे bhāṣadhve
1st	भाषे bhāṣe	भाषावहे bhāṣāvahe	भाषामहे bhāṣāmahe

VOCABULARY

SANSKRIT		ENGLISH
अव + गम्	अवगच्छति	
ava + √gam (active)	**avagacchati**	he understands
उद् + भू	उद्भवति	
ud + √bhū (active)	**udbhavati**	he is born
उद् + स्था	उत्तिष्ठति	
ud + √sthā (active)	**uttiṣṭhati**	he stands up
रम्	रमते	
√ram (middle)	**ramate** -ti	he enjoys
शुभ्	शोभते	
√śubh (middle)	**śobhate** -ti	he shines
स्मि	स्मयते	
√smi (middle)	**smayate** -ti	he smiles

The gerund forms for each of these verbs is listed at the back of the text (pages 312-314).

EXERCISES

1. Memorize the **sandhi** rules that take place when the first word ends in **m**.

2. Memorize the endings for the imperfect middle.

3. Translate the following sentences into English:

a. कथामवगत्य कविरस्मयत ।१।

b. रामः सीता च नद्यां जलमरमेताम् ।२।

c. यदातिथिरुपगच्छति तदा बाला उत्तिष्ठन्ति ।३।

d. यदातिथिरुपागच्छत्तदा बाला उदतिष्ठन् ।४।

e. यत्र शान्तिस्तत्र सुखं ।५।

f. पुत्रिका नृपस्य गृह उद्भवति ।६।

g. विद्ययाविद्यां जित्वा सूर्य इवर्षिः शोभते ।७।

h. अहो राम कथं तस्मिन्गज उत्तिष्ठसीति बालो ऽपृच्छत् ।८।

i. वने फलानि रत्वा वीरस्य पत्नी गृहं प्रत्यगच्छत् ।९।

j. यो बालस्तस्य पुत्रस्तं रामो ऽस्मयत ।१०।

4. Translate the following sentences into Sanskrit:

    a. Since the guest enjoyed the fruit, (therefore) he returns to the house again.

    b. Having smiled, Sītā spoke to the beautiful girl.

    c. Having come from the elephant, he approached that village.

    d. He understands that the man has a son.

    e. Having drank the water from the fruit, the girl stands up.

    f. When the moon shines, then you see shadows in the forest.

    g. When the boy sees the elephant, then he smiles and laughs.

h. The man and his wife enjoy that beautiful house.

i. When his son was born, the hero smiled.

j. The girl obtained fruit from the man who is standing.

16

LESSON SIXTEEN

Alphabet:	The **sandhi** rules for final **n**
Grammar:	Nouns in **an**
	The imperfect for √**as**
	The **dvandva** compound
Vocabulary:	Nouns in **an**
	More adjectives

ALPHABET: SANDHI RULES FOR FINAL N

1. Now we will learn the **sandhi** rules for when the first word ends in **n**. In the majority of cases it remains unchanged. The chart below contains eight rules (a - h) in which **n** changes.

2. For each rule, those letters in the alphabet which are in bold represent the first letter of the second word, which causes the change. The letters outside the alphabet are the change the **n** undergoes. See the examples on the following pages.

preceding **n** becomes								preceding **n** becomes
				a	**ā**			
				i	**ī**			
				u	**ū**			**nn** (e)
				ṛ	**ṝ**			(if preceded by
				ḷ				a short vowel)
				e	**ai**			
				o	**au**			
		ka	kha	ga	gha	na		
(a) **ṃś**		**ca**	**cha**	**ja**	**jha**	ña		**ñ** (f)
(b) **ṃṣ**		**ṭa**	**ṭha**	**ḍa**	**ḍha**	ṇa		**ṇ** (g)
(c) **ṃs**		**ta**	**tha**	da	dha	na		
		pa	pha	ba	bha	ma		
				ya	ra	**la**	va	**ṃl** (h)
(d) **ñ** (ch)	**śa**	ṣa	sa	ha				
		end of line						

3. Here are examples for each of these eight rules:

(a) तस्मिन् + च = तस्मिंश्च

tasmin + ca = tasmiṃś ca

नरान् + च = नरांश्च

narān + ca = narāṃś ca

(b) नरान् + ट = नरांष्ट

narān + ṭa = narāṃṣ ṭa

(c) नरान् + तत्र = नरांस्तत्र

narān + tatra = narāṃs tatra

(d) नरान् + शोभन्ते = नराञ्छोभन्ते

narān + śobhante = narāñ chobhante

or (rarely)

नरान् + शोभन्ते = नराञ्शोभन्ते

narān + śobhante = narāñ śobhante

(e) राजन् + अत्र = राजन्नत्र

rājan + atra = rājann atra

नरान् + अत्र = नरानत्र

narān + atra = narān atra

(f) **नरान् + जयति = नराञ्जयति**

narān + jayati = narāñ jayati

(g) **नरान् + ड = नराण्ड**

narān + ḍa = narāṇ ḍa

(h) **नरान् + लभते = नरांल्लभते**

narān + labhate = narāṃl labhate

GRAMMAR: NOUNS IN AN, COMPOUNDS

1. Here is the declension for nouns ending in **an**:

Stem: **rājan** (masculine) king; **ātman** (masculine) Self

	Singular	Dual	Plural
Nom	राजा rājā	राजानौ rājānau	राजानस् rājānas
Acc	राजानम् rājānam	राजानौ rājānau	राज्ञस् आत्मनस् rājñas/ātmanas
Inst	राज्ञा आत्मना rājñā/ātmanā	राजभ्याम् rājabhyām	राजभिस् rājabhis
Dat	राज्ञे आत्मने rājñe/ātmane	राजभ्याम् rājabhyām	राजभ्यस् rājabhyas
Abl	राज्ञस् आत्मनस् rājñas/ātmanas	राजभ्याम् rājabhyām	राजभ्यस् rājabhyas
Gen	राज्ञस् आत्मनस् rājñas/ātmanas	राज्ञोस् आत्मनोस् rājños/ātmanos	राज्ञाम् आत्मनाम् rājñām/ātmanām
Loc	राज्ञि आत्मनि rājni/ātmani	राज्ञोस् आत्मनोस् rājños/ātmanos	राजसु rājasu
Voc	राजन् rājan	राजानौ rājānau	राजानस् rājānas

2. Note that **rājan** and **ātman** are really the same declension. The only difference is that the **tmn** combination cannot occur, so **ātman** always keeps the **a** before the **n**. Sometimes that **a** may be long. If so, the form is considered strong. The neuter is the same as the masculine, except for the nominative and accusative:

Stem: **nāman** (neuter) name

Nom	नाम **nāma**	नाम्नी नामनी **nāmnī/nāmanī**	नामानि **nāmāni**
Acc	नाम **nāma**	नाम्नी नामनी **nāmnī/nāmanī**	नामानि **nāmāni**
Inst	नाम्ना **nāmnā**	नामभ्याम् **nāmabhyām**	नामभिस् **nāmabhis**
Dat	नाम्ने **nāmne**	नामभ्याम् **nāmabhyām**	नामभ्यस् **nāmabhyas**
Abl	नाम्नस् **nāmnas**	नामभ्याम् **nāmabhyām**	नामभ्यस् **nāmabhyas**
Gen	नाम्नस् **nāmnas**	नाम्नोस् **nāmnos**	नाम्नाम् **nāmnām**
Loc	नाम्नि नामनि **nāmni/nāmani**	नाम्नोस् **nāmnos**	नामसु **nāmasu**
Voc	नामन् नाम **nāman/nāma**	नाम्नी नामनी **nāmnī/nāmanī**	नामानि **nāmāni**

3. Here is the imperfect for √**as**:

	Singular	Dual	Plural
3rd	आसीत् **āsīt**	आस्ताम् **āstām**	आसन् **āsan**
2nd	आसीः **āsīḥ**	आस्तम् **āstam**	आस्त **āsta**
1st	आसम् **āsam**	आस्व **āsva**	आस्म **āsma**

Remember that these are not the endings, but the entire verb.

4. Now we will begin our study of compounds (**samāsa**). Sanskrit has several different types of compounds, which are words joined together to create one unit. In **devanāgarī**, compounds are written without a break. With transliteration, (in this text) the members of a compound are joined by a hyphen, when **sandhi** permits. For example:

   एकवचन **eka-vacana** (singular number)

5. Nominal compounds join nouns, adjectives, or pronouns. They are usually formed by taking the stem form (**nara**, **phala**, etc.) and putting them together, using **sandhi** rules. Generally only the last member is declined, and prior members have loss (**luk**) of case ending (**sup**).

6. The first type of compound that we will study is the **dvandva** compound. A **dvandva** (related to the word "dual") is a series of

equal items that would normally be joined by "and." For example, "Sītā and Rāma" could be written as a **dvandva** compound:

सीतारामौ
sītā-rāmau

7. All compounds may undergo an analysis (**vigraha**), which is how the words would appear if the compound were dissolved. For example:

सीतारामौ	vigraha:	सीता रामश्च
sītā-rāmau		**sītā rāmaś ca**
"Sītā-Rāma"	analysis:	Sītā and Rāma

8. In this **dvandva**, called an **itaretara-dvandva**, the last member is in the dual because two persons are named.

9. If more than two persons are named, the last member is in the plural. For example:

आचार्यशिष्याः	vigraha:	आचार्यः शिष्याश्च
ācārya-śiṣyāḥ		**ācāryaḥ śiṣyāḥ ca**
"teacher-students"	analysis:	the teacher and students

10. A **dvandva** with three members is always plural. For example:

अश्वगजमृगाः	vigraha:	अश्वो गजो मृगाश्च
aśva-gaja-mṛgāḥ		**aśvo gajo mṛgāś ca**
"horse-elephant-deer"	analysis:	horse, elephant and deer

11. The gender is determined by the last item named. For example:

रामसीते	**vigraha**:	रामः सीता च
rāma-sīte		**rāmaḥ sītā ca**
"Rāma-Sīte"	analysis:	Rāma and Sītā

12. The first member is in its stem form even if it refers to something plural. Because of this, there is sometimes ambiguity concerning whether a member is singular, dual, or plural. For example:

आचार्यशिष्याः	could be analyzed as:
"teacher-students"	teacher and students (or)
	teachers and student (or)
	teachers and students

You must judge the correct translation by the context, and in most contexts, the first example would be what is meant: "the teacher and the students."

13. There is an additional kind of **dvandva**, called **samāhāra**, in which the ending is always singular and neuter. The members are referred to collectively as a single unit. Often pairs of opposites are put in **samāhāra-dvandva** form. For example:

सुखदुःखम्	**vigraha**:	सुखं दुःखं च
sukha-duḥkham		**sukhaṃ duḥkhaṃ ca**
"happiness-suffering"	analysis:	happiness and suffering

14. Words ending in **-an** usually act in compounds like words that end in **-a**. For example, **ātman** is often reduced to **ātma**, whether it is at the end or before the end of a compound. For example:

रामराजौ

rāma-rājau	Rāma and the king

राजरामौ

rāja-rāmau	The king and Rāma

15. A noun can be negated by placing **a** before it. This is also considered to be a compound (a **nañ**, or negative **samāsa**). For example:

विद्या	**अविद्या**
vidyā	**avidyā**
knowledge	ignorance

16. If the word begins with a vowel, then it is negated with **an**. A gerund is also negated with **a** or **an**. For example:

अगत्वा

agatvā	not having gone

अनुदित्वा

anuditvā	not having spoken

If the gerund begins with **a** or **an**, and there are no other prefixes, the ending is -**tvā**.

17. There are many additional rules regarding compounds that will be covered in later lessons.

VOCABULARY	SANSKRIT	ENGLISH
	आत्मन् **ātman** (mas)	Self (use capital "S")
	कर्मन् **karman** (neuter)	action
	कृष्ण **kṛṣṇa** mf(**ā**)n (noun or adj)	Kṛṣṇa, black
	नामन् **nāman** (neuter)	name
	प्रिय **priya** mf(**ā**)n (adj)	dear, beloved
	रमणीय **ramaṇīya** mf(**ā**)n (adj)	pleasant
	राजन् **rājan** (mas)	king
	शुक्ल **śukla** mf(**ā**)n (adj)	white
	शोभन **śobhana** mf(**ā** or **ī**)n (adj)	shining, bright, beautiful

EXERCISES

1. Memorize the **sandhi** rules for final **n**.

2. Memorize the masculine and neuter for the **an** declension.

3. Memorize the imperfect of √**as**.

4. Review the formation of **dvandva** compounds.

5. Translate the following sentences into English:

   a. कृष्णो ऽश्वमृगगजानगोपयत् ।१।

   b. प्रियो राजा रामो ग्रामस्य बालानस्मयत ।२।

   c. कन्या प्रजां सूर्यात्तस्याश्छाययागोपयत् ।३।

   d. य आत्मानं बोधति स कर्माणि रमते ।४। (Use plural for "action.")

   e. प्रजा कृष्णस्याश्वस्य कर्माहसत् ।५।

   f. यदा सा तस्य नामावदत्तदा बाल उदतिष्ठत् ।६।

   g. प्रियं तस्य पुत्रमुपगत्य वीरो ऽस्मयत ।७।

h. बालबालौ शोभनस्य राज्ञः प्रजे स्तः ।८।

i. शुक्ला अश्वा वन आसन् ।९।

j. आसीद्राजा रामो नाम ग्रामे ।१०।

6. Translate the following sentences into Sanskrit:

   a. The black horse drinks the water from the river.

   b. He who knows the Self enjoys action and inaction.

   c. The king's name was Kṛṣṇa.

   d. The king enjoys the pleasant actions of the son.

   e. The beloved hero understood success and failure.

   f. The boy comes from the elephant and returns to the house.

   g. That which neither comes nor goes is the Self.

   h. When the king approached, the boys and girls stood up.

   i. The man who was king came from the black forest.

   j. Knowledge of the Self is knowledge also of the sun and the moon.

17

LESSON SEVENTEEN

Alphabet: The **sandhi** rules for final **t**

Grammar: Nouns ending in **ṛ** and the future tense

Vocabulary: Nouns in **ṛ**

ALPHABET: SANDHI RULES FOR FINAL T

1. When the first word ends in **t**, in the majority of cases it remains the same if the following letter is unvoiced, and it changes to **d** if the following letter is voiced. Those letters which are in bold are exceptions. See the examples that follow.

t remains **t** except:									**t** changes to **d** except:
				a	ā				
				i	ī				
				u	ū				
				ṛ	ṝ				
				ḷ					
				e	ai				(before all nasals)
				o	au				**n** (d)
		ka	kha	ga	gha	**na**			
(a) **c**		**ca**	**cha**	**ja**	**jha**	**ña**			**j** (e)
(b) **ṭ**		**ṭa**	**ṭha**	**ḍa**	**ḍha**	**ṇa**			**ḍ** (f)
		ta	tha	da	dha	**na**			
		pa	pha	ba	bha	**ma**			
				ya	ra	**la**	va		**l** (g)
(c) **c** (ch)	**śa**	ṣa	sa	**ha**					**d (dh)** (h)
		end of line							

2. Here are examples for each of these eight rules:

(a) **रामात् + च = रामाच्च**

rāmāt + ca = rāmāc ca

(b) रामात् + ट = रामाट्ट
rāmāt + ṭa = rāmāṭ ṭa

(c) रामात् + शास्त्रम् = रामाच्छास्त्रम्
rāmāt + śāstram = rāmāc chāstram

(d) रामात् + मन्यते = रामान्मन्यते
rāmāt + manyate = rāmān manyate

(e) रामात् + जलम् = रामाज्जलम्
rāmāt + jalam = rāmāj jalam

(f) रामात् + ड = रामाड्ड
rāmāt + ḍa = rāmāḍ ḍa

(g) रामात् + लभते = रामाल्लभते
rāmāt + labhate = rāmāl labhate

(h) रामात् + हस्तः = रामाद्धस्तः
rāmāt + hastaḥ = rāmād dhastaḥ

GRAMMAR: NOUNS ENDING IN Ṛ AND THE FUTURE TENSE

1. Here is the declension for nouns ending in **ṛ**. These nouns are usually an agent of action or a relation, such as father or mother. Stem: **dātṛ** (masculine) giver; **svasṛ** (feminine) sister

	Singular	Dual	Plural
Nom	दाता **dātā**	दातारौ **dātārau**	दातारस् **dātāras**
Acc	दातारम् **dātāram**	दातारौ **dātārau**	दातॄन् स्वसॄस् **dātṝn / svasṝs**
Inst	दात्रा **dātrā**	दातृभ्याम् **dātṛbhyām**	दातृभिस् **dātṛbhis**
Dat	दात्रे **dātre**	दातृभ्याम् **dātṛbhyām**	दातृभ्यस् **dātṛbhyas**
Abl	दातुस् **dātus**	दातृभ्याम् **dātṛbhyām**	दातृभ्यस् **dātṛbhyas**
Gen	दातुस् **dātus**	दात्रोस् **dātros**	दातॄणाम् **dātṝṇām**
Loc	दातरि **dātari**	दात्रोस् **dātros**	दातृषु **dātṛṣu**
Voc	दातर् **dātar**	दातारौ **dātārau**	दातारस् **dātāras**

2. Father, mother, and brother have a weaker form (looking at the second syllable) in the nominative dual and plural, and the accusative:

Stem: **pitṛ** (mas) father; **mātṛ** (fem) mother; **bhrātṛ** (mas) brother

Nom	पिता **pitā**	पितरौ **pitarau**	पितरस् **pitaras**
Acc	पितरम् **pitaram**	पितरौ **pitarau**	पितॄन् भ्रातॄन् मातॄस् **pitṝn bhrātṝn mātṝs**

3. In a few but common **dvandva** compounds of pairs, such as "mother and father," the first word usually ends in **ā**. For example:

मातापितरौ
mātā-pitarau
mother and father

4. Now we will study the future tense. Sometimes the present indicative may indicate the immediate future. For example:

gacchāmi I will go

5. More often, the simple future is used. The future tense (**lṛṭ**) is formed by adding **sya** or **iṣya** to the strengthened root. Roots are strengthened by adding **guṇa** or **vṛddhi** changes to the vowel (see page 167).

6. Here is the third person singular future for some of the verbs we have learned:

upa + √gam	upagamiṣyati	he will approach
√gam	gamiṣyati	he will go
√gup	gopayiṣyati	he will protect
√ji	jeṣyati	he will conquer
√dṛś	drakṣyati	he will see
√nī	neṣyati	he will lead
√paṭh	paṭhiṣyati	he will read
√paś	drakṣyati	he will see
√pā	pāsyati	he will drink
√prach	prakṣyati	he will ask
√budh	bodhiṣyati	he will know
√bhū	bhaviṣyati	he will be
√man	maṃsyate	he will think
√ram	raṃsyate	he will enjoy

√labh	lapsyate	he will obtain
√vad	vadiṣyati	he will speak
√vas	vatsyati	he will live
√śubh	śobhiṣyati	he will shine
√sev	seviṣyate	he will serve
√sthā	sthāsyati	he will stand
√smi	smeṣyate	he will smile
√smṛ	smariṣyati	he will remember
√has	hasiṣyati	he will laugh

VOCABULARY: NOUNS IN Ṛ

SANSKRIT		ENGLISH
कदा	**kadā** (indeclinable)	when (used like **kutra**)
कर्तृ	**kartṛ** (mas)	maker, doer
कर्त्री	**kartrī** (fem)	maker, doer (follows long **ī** declension)
कुलम्	**kulam** (neuter)	family
दातृ	**dātṛ** (mas)	giver
दात्री	**dātrī** (fem)	giver
पितृ	**pitṛ** (mas)	father
भ्रातृ	**bhrātṛ** (mas)	brother
मातृ	**mātṛ** (fem)	mother
स्वसृ	**svasṛ** (fem)	sister

EXERCISES

1. Memorize the **sandhi** rules for final **t**.

2. Memorize the declension for nouns ending in **ṛ**.

3. Make yourself familiar with the future third person singular forms.

4. Translate the following sentences into English:

   a. मम पिता तत्र गमिष्यतीति बालस्तस्य मातरमवदत् ।१।

   b. कदा तव भ्राता जलं लप्स्यत इति पितापृच्छत् ।२।

   c. पितामातरौ जलात्कुलं गोपयिष्यतः ।३।

   d. कदा वनादागमिष्यसीति रामस्तस्य भ्रातरमपृच्छत् ।४।

   e. तस्य पितरं सेवित्वा रामो राजा भविष्यति ।५।

f. यदा तस्या भ्रातरं मन्यते तदा सा स्मयते ।६।

g. माता तस्याः प्रजायै सुखस्य दात्री भवति ।७।

h. य आत्मानं जयति स शान्तेः कर्ता ।८।

i. जलं पीत्वा तस्य मातुः पुस्तकं पठिष्यति ।९।

j. भ्रात्रा सह रामो वने वत्स्यति ।१०।

5. Translate the following sentences into Sanskrit:

   a. When my sister was born, she smiled at my mother.

   b. My family's name is from the name of a seer.

   c. "When will I speak to the king?" her father thought.

   d. Her father's wife is her mother.

   e. My father is the maker of peace in our family.

   f. The brother and sister will obtain fruit from the forest.

g. The hero will protect the king from the fire in the forest.

h. The son of the king has no brothers.

i. When will the students obtain knowledge from the virtuous teacher?

j. "I have seen you in the pond," the king says to the beautiful son.

18

LESSON EIGHTEEN

Alphabet:	All remaining **sandhi** rules
Grammar:	Nouns in **u** The **karmadhāraya** and **tatpuruṣa** compound
Vocabulary:	Nouns in **u**, more adjectives

ALPHABET: ALL REMAINING SANDHI RULES

1. We will now study the remaining **sandhi** rules, which include final **r**, **p**, **ṭ**, **k**, **ṅ**, and initial **ch**.

2. Here are the rules for final **r**:

   (a) Before a word beginning with a voiced letter, the **r** remains the same. For example:

   पुनर् + गच्छति = पुनर्गच्छति
   punar + gacchati = punar gacchati

   पुनर् + आगच्छति = पुनरागच्छति
   punar + āgacchati = punar āgacchati

   (b) Before an unvoiced letter or the end of a line, **r** follows the same rules as final **s**. For example:

   पुनर् + पुनर् = पुनः पुनः
   punar + punar = punaḥ punaḥ

   पुनर् + तत्र = पुनस्तत्र
   punar + tatra = punas tatra

   (c) Final **r**, whether original or derived from **s**, cannot stand before another **r**. The final **r** is dropped and the vowel before it made long if it is short. For example:

   पुनर् + रामस् = पुना रामः
   punar + rāmas = punā rāmaḥ

3. Here are the rules for final **p**, **ṭ**, and **k**:

   (a) Before a voiced sound these letters become voiced, and before an unvoiced sound they remain the same. For example:

   ऋक् + **वेद्** = **ऋग्वेद्**

   ṛk + veda = ṛg veda

   ऋक् + **संहिता** = **ऋक्संहिता**

   ṛk + saṃhitā = ṛk saṃhitā

   (b) Before a nasal these letters become the nasal of their row (**varga**). For example:

   सुप् + **नाम** = **सुम्नाम**

   sup + nāma = sumnāma

   (c) Before **h** these letters become voiced and the **h** becomes their voiced aspirated counterpart. For example:

   वाक् + **हसति** = **वाग्घसति**

   vāk + hasati = vāg ghasati

4. Here is the rule for final **n̄**:

   (a) Like final **n**, final **n̄** becomes **n̄n̄** before vowels if the **n̄** is preceded by a short vowel.

5. Here is the rule for initial **ch**:

   (a) Initial **ch** becomes **cch** if the first word ends in a short vowel. The **ch** also becomes **cch** after the preposition **ā** and **mā**. For example:

कुत्र + छाया = कुत्र च्छाया

kutra + chāyā = kutra cchāyā

6. Ambiguities can sometimes be created by **sandhi**. Two different sets of words could appear the same after **sandhi** has been applied. For example:

रामस् + एव = राम एव

rāmas + eva = rāma eva

रामे + एव = राम एव

rāme + eva = rāma eva

बालास् + न = बाला न

bālās + na = bālā na

बाला + न = बाला न

bālā + na = bālā na

You can usually judge from the context of the sentence which words are correct.

GRAMMAR:
NOUNS IN U,
MORE COMPOUNDS

1. Here is the declension for final **u**:

Stem: **hetu** (masculine) cause; **dhenu** (feminine) cow

Nom	हेतुस् **hetus**	हेतू **hetū**	हेतवस् **hetavas**
Acc	हेतुम् **hetum**	हेतू **hetū**	हेतून् धेनूस् **hetūn / dhenūs**
Inst	हेतुना धेन्वा **hetunā/dhenvā**	हेतुभ्याम् **hetubhyām**	हेतुभिस् **hetubhis**
Dat	हेतवे धेन्वै **hetave (dhenvai)**	हेतुभ्याम् **hetubhyām**	हेतुभ्यस् **hetubhyas**
Abl	हेतोस् धेन्वास् **hetos (dhenvās)**	हेतुभ्याम् **hetubhyām**	हेतुभ्यस् **hetubhyas**
Gen	हेतोस् धेन्वास् **hetos (dhenvās)**	हेत्वोस् **hetvos**	हेतूनाम् **hetūnām**
Loc	हेतौ धेन्वाम् **hetau (dhenvām)**	हेत्वोस् **hetvos**	हेतुषु **hetuṣu**
Voc	हेतो **heto**	हेतू **hetū**	हेतवस् **hetavas**

The singular dative, ablative, genitive, and locative have an optional feminine form. For example, the feminine dative singular is **dhenave** or **dhenvai**. The feminine instrumental singular is **dhenvā**. This entire declension is the same as the declension ending in **i** (page 160). The only differences are due to **sandhi**.

2. Now we will study another kind of compound: the **tatpuruṣa** compound. Unlike the **dvandva**, whose members are considered equal, in the **tatpuruṣa** the last member is usually principal (**pradhāna**) and the prior member is subordinate (**upasarjana**). The subordinate member determines the sense of the principal member, and so the **tatpuruṣa** is called a "determinative compound." The last word is grammatically independent.

3. One type of **tatpuruṣa** is the **karmadhāraya**. In a **karmadhāraya** compound, both words refer to the same object, and if separated, would be in the same case (**samānādhikaraṇa**).

4. The simplest kind of **karmadhāraya** is the adjective and noun:

शुक्लमाला	**vigraha**:	शुक्ला माला
śukla-mālā		**śuklā mālā**
"white-garland"	analysis:	the white garland
प्रियबालात्	**vigraha**:	प्रियाद्बालात्
priya-bālāt		**priyād bālāt**
"from dear-boy"	analysis:	from the dear boy

Note that even if the second member of the compound is a feminine noun (**mālā**), the adjective often takes the form of a masculine stem (**a**).

5. Another type of **karmadhāraya** is the noun and noun:

राजर्षिः	**vigraha**:	राजर्षिः
rāja-ṛṣiḥ		**rāja ṛṣiḥ**
"king-seer"	analysis:	the king seer

6. In other **tatpuruṣa** compounds (here usually referred to as **tatpuruṣa**), the members refer to different objects and would be in different cases (**vyadhikaraṇa**) if the compound were dissolved. The compound is further named after the case of the first member, which would be in cases two through seven if the compound were analyzed. For example, if the first member is genitive, the compound is called a genitive **tatpuruṣa**. Here are two genitive **tatpuruṣa** compounds:

रामपुत्रः	**vigraha**:	रामस्य पुत्रः
rāma-putraḥ		**rāmasya putraḥ**
"Rāma-son"	analysis:	the son of Rāma

नरपुस्तकम्	**vigraha**:	नरस्य पुस्तकम्
nara-pustakam		**narasya pustakam**
"man-book"	analysis:	the man's book

7. A compound may, like a simple word, become a member in another compound. In these cases, the analysis usually begins with the larger pieces, of which some pieces may be compounds subject to further analysis. For example:

रामपुत्रपुस्तकम्
rāma-putra-pustakam
"Rāma-son-book" — Here the analysis begins with the last two members:

(1) रामपुत्रस्य पुस्तकम्
rāma-putrasya pustakam
"Rāma-son's" book — The first two members are then analyzed:

(2) **रामस्य पुत्रः**

rāmasya putraḥ

the son of Rāma

(3) **रामस्य पुत्रस्य पुस्तकम्**

rāmasya putrasya pustakam

the book of the son of Rāma

In India, rather than "taking apart" a compound, the analysis starts with smaller units and shows how the compound is "built up."

8. Compounds may be classified into four groups. The following is a generalized description to which exceptions may be added later:

(1) **dvandva**. In this compound, each member has equal significance—each member is considered principal. There are two types:

(a) **itaretara**. The members are viewed separately. For example, **rāma-sīte**, "Rāma and Sītā."

(b) **samāhāra**. The members are viewed as a whole. For example, **sukha-duḥkham**, "happiness and suffering."

(2) **tatpuruṣa**. In this compound, the first member qualifies and is subordinate to the second member. There are several types:

(a) **tatpuruṣa (vyadhikaraṇa-tatpuruṣa)**. This name is normally used for the compound that refers to different objects. The first member would be in a different case than the second if the compound were dissolved. There are six types of this compound, corresponding to cases two through seven. For example, **rāma-putraḥ**, "the son of Rāma."

(b) **nañ**. This is a **tatpuruṣa** compound that begins with **a** or **an**, used to negate. For example, **avidyā**, "ignorance."

(c) **karmadhāraya (samānādhikaraṇa-tatpuruṣa)**. Both members refer to the same object and therefore would be in the same case if the compound were dissolved. For example, **śukla-mālā**, "the white garland." If the first member is a number, it is called a **dvigu**. For example, **dvi-vacana**, "dual number."

(f) **upapada**. The second member is an adjusted verbal root. For example, **brahma-vit**, "the knower of **brahman**."

(3) **bahuvrīhi**. In this compound, the actual principal is outside of the compound. The compound serves as an adjective, describing something else. The members may be in the same or different cases. For example, **mahā-rathaḥ**, "Great chariot," means one whose chariot is great, or a "great hero." To use an example in English, "redcoat" refers to a person whose coat is red.

(4) **avyayībhāva**. This compound begins with an indeclinable For example, **anu-bhandam**, "proper order, sequence."

9. These four groups of compounds may be understood from the perspective of which member is principal:

(1) **dvandva**	Both members are principal.
(2) **tatpuruṣa**	Second member is principal.
(3) **bahuvrīhi**	Neither member is principal.
(4) **avyayībhāva**	First member is principal.

10. If pronouns are used as prior members of a compound, they are put in base forms, which are used regardless of the case, gender, or number of the pronoun:

mad	I
asmad	we
tvad	you
yuṣmad	you (plural)
tad	he, she, it, they

For example:

मद्बालः
mad-bālaḥ
my boy (genitive **tatpuruṣa**)

तत्पुरुष
tat-puruṣa
his man (genitive **tatpuruṣa**)

VOCABULARY	SANSKRIT		ENGLISH
	अल्प	**alpa** mf(**ā**)n (adj)	little
	गुरु	**guru** (mas noun) mf(vī)n (adj)	teacher, heavy
	धेनु	**dhenu** (fem)	cow
	पूर्ण	**pūrṇa** mf(**ā**)n (adj)	full
	बहु	**bahu** mf (**vī** or **u**)n (adj)	much, many
	शत्रु	**śatru** (mas)	enemy
	शीघ्र	**śīghra** mf(**ā**)n (adj)	swift
	हेतु	**hetu** (mas)	cause, motive

EXERCISES

1. Memorize the last of the **sandhi** rules.

2. Memorize the declension for **u**.

3. Review how to form **karmadhāraya** and **tatpuruṣa** compounds and memorize the short forms of the pronouns used in those compounds.

4. Translate the following sentences into English:

   a. शुक्लधेनुर्वाप्यां तिष्ठति जलं च पिबति ।१।

   b. ऋषिः शत्रुमजयत् ।२।

   c. यदि वनं फलस्य पूर्णमस्ति तदा धेनवस्तत्र गच्छन्ति ।३।

   d. मत्मातात्पं पुस्तकं पठति तं रमते च ।४।

   e. गुरुर्बहुसुखं दाता ।५।

   f. अल्पबालः शुक्लसूर्य इव शोभते ।६।

g. यदात्मानमवगच्छसि तदा त्वं बहुसुखस्य
हेतुरसि ।७।

h. कदा रमणीयराजा शत्रोरस्माकं कुलं गोपयिष्यति ।८।

i. शीघ्रा बाला फलेन सह वनादागच्छति ।९।

j. हेतुर्गुरोः सुखं तस्य शिष्याणां सिद्ध्य भवति ।१०।

5. Translate the following sentences into Sanskrit:

   a. The beautiful little cow drank water from the pond.

   b. The swift black horse stands in the little village.

   c. Having conquered the enemy, the army will enjoy peace and happiness.

   d. Ignorance is the enemy of truth.

   e. Having known the Self, he understood the cause of action and inaction.

f. The child was born in a little house in the beautiful forest.

g. The student will bring the beautiful garland for his teacher.

h. The forest is full of fruit and the pond is full of water.

i. Seeing his family, the father went to the forest for water.

j. When will the beautiful cow come here from the swift river?

LESSON ONE

5.
a. You ask and he goes.
b. I go and I ask. (or) I go and ask.
c. He asks and he goes. (or) He asks and goes.
d. You go and I ask.
e. He asks and I ask. (or) He and I ask.
f. You go and he goes. (or) You and he go.
g. I ask and you go.
h. He asks and I go.

6.
a. **gacchāmi pṛcchāmi ca** (or) **gacchāmi ca pṛcchāmi ca**
b. **pṛcchasi gacchati ca** (**ca** may also go in the middle.)
c. **pṛcchati gacchasi ca**
d. **gacchati pṛcchati ca**
e. **pṛcchasi**
f. **pṛcchāmi ca gacchasi ca** (or) **pṛcchāmi gacchasi ca**
g. **gacchāmi gacchasi ca**
h. **gacchati gacchasi ca**

LESSON TWO

5. a. Where do we two live?
   b. You are and we two are.
   c. I live and they two remember.
   d. You two ask and he remembers.
   e. Where are we two going?
   f. Where am I?
   g. Where am I going? (or) Where do I go?
   h. I ask and he remembers.
   i. You live and we two go.
   j. Where are you going? (or) Where do you go?

6. Use only one verb. The auxiliary verb "are" need not be translated when there is another verb.

   (Just observe the sentences in parentheses, written with the **sandhi** included.)

   a. **kutra gacchathaḥ**
      (**kutra gacchathaḥ**)
   b. **vasāmi vasataḥ ca**
      (**vasāmi vasataś ca**)
   c. **pṛcchāvaḥ smarataḥ ca**
      (**pṛcchāvaḥ smarataś ca**)
   d. **gacchasi gacchati ca**
      (**gacchasi gacchati ca**)

LESSON TWO (CONTINUED)

e. **kutra gacchāmi**

(kutra gacchāmi)

f. **bhavāmi ca bhavathaḥ ca**

(bhavāmi ca bhavathaś ca)

g. **kutra bhavasi**

(kutra bhavasi)

h. **kutra gacchati**

(kutra gacchati)

LESSON THREE

5. a. He speaks and I do not speak. (or) He says and I do not say.
   b. You two speak and those two remember.
   c. They do not go.
   d. We all stand and go.
   e. You two are and you two live. (or) You two are and live.
   f. Where are you?
   g. They stand and go. (or) They stand and they go.
   h. He does not ask and he does not speak.

6. (All the following sentences are written the same with **sandhi**.)

   a **kutra gacchanti**

   b. **na vadāmaḥ**

   c. **pṛcchati ca vadanti ca**

   d. **kutra tiṣṭhāmaḥ**

   e. **kutra vasataḥ**

   f. **na gacchāmaḥ**

   g. **pṛcchāmi smaranti ca**

   h. **kutra bhavāmaḥ**

LESSON FOUR

4. a. The men remember the deer.
   b. Rāma goes to the two horses.
   c. Where do the elephants live?
   d. The two men speak to Rāma.
   e. The son remembers or asks.
   f. Rāma goes to the deer.
   g. The two horses do not speak.
   h. Rāma speaks to the son.

5. (The sentences in parentheses are with **sandhi**.)
   a. **narās mṛgam vadanti**

      (narā mṛgaṃ vadanti)
   b. **rāmas aśvān vadati**

      (rāmo 'śvān vadati)
   c. **putras aśvam gacchati tiṣṭhati ca**

      (putro 'śvaṃ gacchati tiṣṭhati ca)
   d. **gajās na smaranti**

      (gajā na smaranti)
   e. **kutra aśvās tiṣṭhanti**

      (kutra aśvās tiṣṭhanti)
   f. **kutra gajas bhavati**

      (kutra gajo bhavati)

LESSON FOUR (CONTINUED)

g. **rāmas vadati putras ca smarati**

(rāmo vadati putraś ca smarati)

h. **tiṣṭhanti vā gacchanti vā**

(tiṣṭhanti vā gacchanti vā)

i. **kutra rāmas tiṣṭhati**

(kutra rāmas tiṣṭhati)

j. **rāmas putras vā gacchati**

(rāmaḥ putro vā gacchati)

k. **rāmas putras ca gacchataḥ**

(rāmaḥ putraś ca gacchataḥ)

6. a. The two men speak to the son.
   b. Where are the horses and elephants going?
   c. The horse or the deer goes.
   d. Rāma speaks to the two sons.
   e. The deer, horse and elephant are going.
   f. The sons do not remember the deer. (Deer is plural.)
   g. Where do the two men live?
   h. I ask Rāma.
   i. The two men do not speak to the sons.
   j. Where are the deer?

LESSON FOUR (CONTINUED)

7. a. **kutra rāmas gacchati**
   (kutra rāmo gacchati)
   b. **rāmas aśvam gacchati**
   (rāmo 'śvaṃ gacchati)
   c. **putras aśvān na vadati**
   (putro 'śvān na vadati)
   d. **gajau naram smarataḥ**
   (gajau naraṃ smarataḥ)
   e. **kutra mṛgau vasataḥ**
   (kutra mṛgau vasataḥ)
   f. **aśvam gacchasi**
   (aśvaṃ gacchasi)
   g. **kutra tiṣṭhāmaḥ**
   (kutra tiṣṭhāmaḥ)
   h. **putras aśvān gajān ca gacchati**
   (putro 'śvān gajāṃś ca gacchati)
   i. **gajam vadatha**
   (gajaṃ vadatha)
   j. **gajas na smarati**
   (gajo na smarati)

LESSON FIVE

4. a. Where do the heroes stand?

   b. There, with the elephant, are the two boys.

   c. The king goes to the horse.

   d. With the horse, the hero goes to the kings.

   e. Rāma lives with the deer.

   f. The boys go with the elephants.

   g. The men speak to the son.

   h. The heroes ask Rāma about all the deer.

   i. The boy goes there for the king.

5. a. **bālās aśvān gacchanti**

   (bālā aśvān gacchanti)

   b. **putras mṛgam nṛpam pṛcchati**

   (putro mṛgaṃ nṛpaṃ pṛcchati)

   c. **nṛpas naram smarati**

   (nṛpo naraṃ smarati)

   d. **putreṇa saha vīras vasati**

   (putreṇa saha vīro vasati)

   e. **bālas nṛpam pṛcchati nṛpas ca smarati**

   (bālo nṛpaṃ pṛcchati nṛpaś ca smarati)

   f. **putreṇa saha tatra gajās na bhavanti**

   (putreṇa saha tatra gajā na bhavanti)

LESSON FIVE

(CONTINUED)

g. **kutra rāmas vasati**

(kutra rāmo vasati)

h. **nṛpas vīras vā bālam vadati**

(nṛpo vīro vā bālaṃ vadati)

i. **vīras bālāya gacchati**

(vīro bālāya gacchati)

j. **tatra gajās aśvais saha bhavanti**

(tatra gajā aśvaiḥ saha bhavanti)

k. **nṛpam smarāmi**

(nṛpaṃ smarāmi)

l. **tatra bālena saha gacchasi**

(tatra bālena saha gacchasi)

6. a. The hero goes with the horses.

   b. The men go there for the king.

   c. The two heroes stand and speak.

   d. All the deer live there.

   e. Where does the king go with the two boys?

   f. Rāma asks the son about the horse.

   g. The elephants are not standing there.

   h. The hero speaks to the boy about the king.

   i. The elephant lives with the deer and the horses.

   j. Where are we standing?

LESSON FIVE (CONTINUED)

7. a. **tatra bālābhyām saha nṛpas vasati**
(tatra bālābhyāṃ saha nṛpo vasati)

b. **kutra gajais saha gacchasi**
(kutra gajaiḥ saha gacchasi)

c. **tatra naras aśvāya gacchati**
(tatra naro 'śvāya gacchati)

d. **bālas nṛpam na smarati**
(bālo nṛpaṃ na smarati)

e. **gajau nṛpam vadāmi**
(gajau nṛpaṃ vadāmi)

f. **nṛpas putrāya aśvam gacchati**
(nṛpaḥ putrāya aśvaṃ gacchati)

g. **kutra tiṣṭhāmaḥ**
(kutra tiṣṭhāmaḥ)

h. **naras aśvam bālam pṛcchati**
(naro 'śvaṃ bālaṃ pṛcchati)

i. **tatra rāmas narāya gacchati**
(tatra rāmo narāya gacchati)

j. **kutra mṛgās bhavanti**
(kutra mṛgā bhavanti)

LESSON SIX

3. a. इति g. भवावः m. ऋषि
   b. नर h. वदसि n. देवता
   c. राम i. नृपस् o. गुण
   d. गज j. न p. जय
   e. वीर k. वा q. गुरु
   f. वसति l. च r. देव

4. a. The boy's elephant goes to the village.
   b. The son of Rāma goes to the horse.
   c. "Here is the horse," the king says.
   d. The son comes from the village.
   e. "Where are the elephants standing?" the king asks.
   f. The boy goes to the village of the king.
   g. "The heroes live here," the men say.
   h. "Where are you going?" asks Rāma.

5. a. **atra vasāmi iti putras vadati**

   (atra vasāmīti putro vadati)

   b. **aśvās gajās ca grāmāt āgacchanti**

   (aśvā gajāś ca grāmād āgacchanti)

LESSON SIX (CONTINUED)

c. **narān smarasi iti nṛpas bālam pṛcchati**
(narān smarasīti nṛpo bālaṃ pṛcchati)
(The question is understood.)

d. **grāmam gacchāmi iti rāmas vadati**
(grāmaṃ gacchāmīti rāmo vadati)

e. **bālāya grāmam gacchāmi iti rāmas vadati**
(bālāya grāmaṃ gacchāmīti rāmo vadati)

f. **kutra vīras gacchati**
(kutra vīro gacchati)

g. **vīras grāmam gacchati iti nṛpas vadati**
(vīro grāmaṃ gacchatīti nṛpo vadati)

h. **atra nṛpasya putras vasati**
(atra nṛpasya putro vasati)

i. **nṛpasya putrās grāmāt āgacchanti**
(nṛpasya putrā grāmād āgacchanti)

j. **naras gajān rāmam vadati**
(naro gajān rāmaṃ vadati)

6. a. The two men come from the village.
b. "Here I am," the boy says to the king.
c. "Where do you live?" the hero asks the son.
d. "I live here with Rāma," the son says.
e. The sons of the man are standing there.

LESSON SIX

(CONTINUED)

f. Here are the hero's hands.

g. "Do you remember Rāma?"the boys ask the man.

h. "Where is the village?" the man asks the son.

i. "The village is there," the son says to the man.

j. "I am going to the village for the elephant," the man says.

7\. a. **kutra gacchasi iti nṛpas bālam pṛcchati**
(kutra gacchasīti nṛpo bālaṃ pṛcchati)

b. **aśvam gacchāmi iti bālas vadati**
(aśvaṃ gacchāmīti bālo vadati)

c. **grāmāṇām nṛpas narān vadati**
(grāmāṇāṃ nṛpo narān vadati)

d. **aśvāt gajāt ca bālau āgacchataḥ**
(aśvād gajāc ca bālāvāgacchataḥ)

e. **rāmeṇa saha bālas vasati**
(rāmeṇa saha bālo vasati)

f. **atra rāmasya putrās bhavanti iti vīras vadati**
(atra rāmasya putrā bhavantīti vīro vadati)

g. **tatra bālās tiṣṭhanti iti nṛpas vadati**
(tatra bālās tiṣṭhantīti nṛpo vadati)

h. **grāmam gacchāmi iti vīrasya putras vadati**
(grāmaṃ gacchāmīti vīrasya putro vadati)

i. **atra mṛgābhyām saha aśvau āgacchataḥ**
(atra mṛgābhyāṃ sahāśvāvāgacchataḥ)

j. **tatra nṛpasya hastau bhavataḥ**
(tatra nṛpasya hastau bhavataḥ)

LESSON SEVEN

1.
a.	**purāṇa**	e.	**gacchati**	i.	**aśva**
b.	**gandharva**	f.	**candra**	j.	**putrasya**
c.	**chandas**	g.	**jyotiṣa**	k.	**śiṣyas**
d.	**vyākaraṇa**	h.	**kalpa**	l.	**tiṣṭhanti**

3.
a. the men (mas, nom, pl)
b. the hands (mas, nom, dual or mas, acc, dual)
c. of the boys (mas, gen, pl)
d. from the king (mas, abl, sing)
e. for Rāma (mas, dat, sing)
f. with the deer (mas, inst, sing)
g. with the elephants (mas, inst, pl)
h. the heroes (mas, acc, pl)
i. in the villages (mas, loc, pl)
j. for the teacher (mas, dat, sing)

4.
a. The student sees the moon and the sun.
b. Oh Rāma! The elephants are standing in the village.
c. "The hero lives in the village," the teacher tells the student.
d. "Where is the moon?" the son asks.
e. The two boys are standing there on the elephant.
f. "Son, where is the moon?" the hero asks the boy.
g. The student of the teacher stands and speaks.
h. Without Rāma the heroes come from the village.
i. The hero's boy thinks that he lives in the village.

LESSON SEVEN (CONTINUED)

5. a. **bālās grāmam gacchanti iti nṛpas vīram vadati**
   (bālā grāmaṃ gacchantīti nṛpo vīraṃ vadati)

   b. **nṛpeṇa vinā bālās āgacchanti**
   (nṛpeṇa vinā bālā āgacchanti)

   c. **vīrasya haste putras bhavati**
   (vīrasya haste putro bhavati)

   d. **kutra bhavāmi iti bālas cintayati**
   (kutra bhavāmīti bālaś cintayati)

   e. **kutra narās bhavanti iti vīrasya putram pṛcchati**
   (kutra narā bhavantīti vīrasya putraṃ pṛcchati)

   f. **sūryas candras na bhavati iti ācāryas śiṣyam vadati**
   (sūryaś candro na bhavatītyācāryaḥ śiṣyaṃ vadati)

   g. **grāme nṛpas vasati**
   (grāme nṛpo vasati)

   h. **tatra nṛpasya gajās bhavanti**
   (tatra nṛpasya gajā bhavanti)

6. a. The boy goes to the village without Rāma.
   b. Where are the king's elephants?
   c. "Here I am," the boy says to the man.
   d. Without the sun you cannot see the moon.
   e. The teacher speaks to the students.

LESSON SEVEN (CONTINUED)

f. "I see the moon," the boy thinks.

g. Here comes the king of the villages.

h. The king sees the hands of the hero.

i. "Where are the sun and the moon?" the boy asks.

j. The students do not remember the man.

7. a. कुत्र गच्छसि इति बालस् नृपस्य पुत्रम् पृच्छति ।

kutra gacchasi iti bālas nṛpasya putram pṛcchati
(kutra gacchasīti bālo nṛpasya putraṃ pṛcchati)

b. मृगौ ग्रामे भवतः ।

mṛgau grāme bhavataḥ
(mṛgau grāme bhavataḥ)

c. आचार्यस् वीरस्य पुत्रम् वदति ।

ācāryas vīrasya putram vadati
(ācāryo vīrasya putraṃ vadati)

d. नृपस् सूर्यम् चन्द्रम् च पश्यति ।

nṛpas sūryam candram ca paśyati
(nṛpaḥ sūryaṃ candraṃ ca paśyati)

e. सूर्येण विना चन्द्रम् न पश्यामः ।

sūryeṇa vinā candram na paśyāmaḥ
(sūryeṇa vinā candraṃ na paśyāmaḥ)

LESSON SEVEN
(CONTINUED)

f. वीरस् नृपस्य गजे भवति ।
vīras nṛpasya gaje bhavati
(vīro nṛpasya gaje bhavati)

g. ग्रामेषु वसामः इति बालास् वदन्ति ।
grāmeṣu vasāmaḥ iti bālās vadanti
(grāmeṣu vasāma iti bālā vadanti)

h. रामस् अश्वेभ्यस् गजान् गच्छति ।
rāmas aśvebhyas gajān gacchati
(rāmo 'śvebhyo gajān gacchati)

i. कुत्र गच्छावः इति बालस् नृपम् पृच्छति ।
kutra gacchāvaḥ iti bālas nṛpam pṛcchati
(kutra gacchāva iti bālo nṛpaṃ pṛcchati)

j. शिष्यैस् सह ग्रामे आचार्यस् वसति ।
śiṣyais saha grāme ācāryas vasati
(śiṣyaiḥ saha grāma ācāryo vasati)

LESSON SEVEN (CONTINUED)

8.

1. **ṛṣi** (seer)
2. **āsana** (seat)
3. **ahaṃkāra** (ego, "I maker")
4. **guṇa** (quality)
5. **jñāna** (knowledge)
6. **kuru-kṣetra** (field of the Kurus)
7. **karma** (action)
8. **dhyāna** (meditation)
9. **darśana** (vision, or system of philosophy)
10. **duḥkha** (pain)
11. **veda** (knowledge)
12. **citta** (mind)
13. **citta-vṛtti** (excitation of mind)
14. **avidyā** (ignorance)
15. **avyakta** (unseen)
16. **dhāraṇa** (focus)
17. **ātman** (the Self)
18. **ānanda** (bliss)
19. **aṣṭāṅga-yoga** (eight limbs of yoga)
20. **tat tvam asi** (thou art that)
21. **nāma-rūpa** (name and form)
22. **upaniṣad** (sit down near)
23. **nitya** (eternal)
24. **dharma** (duty, or that which upholds)

LESSON EIGHT

2. a. पुत्रेणात्र
   b. सहाचार्यस्
   c. तत्रेति
   d. इत्यत्र
   e. इत्याचार्यस्
   f. देवावागच्छतः
   g. नरे ऽत्र
   h. वन इति
   i. फलानीति
   j. स्मरत्यत्र

3. a. gacchati iti
   b. gajau āgacchataḥ
   c. pṛcchati āgacchati ca
   d. gacchāmi iti
   e. haste iti
   f. nṛpasya aśvas
   g. aśve atra
   h. kutra aśvas
   i. kutra iti
   j. gacchati atra

5. a. Rāma goes from the village to the forest.
   b. Immortality is the fruit of knowledge.
   c. "Knowledge is truth," the boys read in the scripture.
   d. "You are the sons of immortality," the teacher tells the students.
   e. How do the teachers remember the hymns?
   f. Rāma says that he sees the truth in the scriptures.

LESSON EIGHT (CONTINUED)

g. Where is the knowledge of the hymns?" the hero asks the son.

h. The king reads the book to the boy.

6. a. **gajas vanasya nṛpas na bhavati**
gajas vanasya nṛpas na bhavati (with vowel **sandhi**)

गजस् वनस्य नृपस् न भवति । (with vowel **sandhi**)

(गजो वनस्य नृपो न भवति ।) (complete **sandhi**)

b. **katham candram paśyasi**
katham candram paśyasi

कथम् चन्द्रम् पश्यसि ।

(कथं चन्द्रं पश्यसि ।) (with complete **sandhi**)

c. **mṛgam paśyāmi iti rāmas cintayati**
mṛgam paśyāmīti rāmas cintayati

मृगम् पश्यामीति रामस् चिन्तयति ।

(मृगं पश्यामीति रामश्चिन्तयति ।)

d. **phalam bālasya hastayos bhavati** (or **phalāni**)
phalam bālasya hastayos bhavati

फलम् बालस्य हस्तयोस् भवति ।

(फलं बालस्य हस्तयोर्भवति ।)

LESSON EIGHT
(CONTINUED)

e. **katham rāmeṇa vinā nṛpas vasati**
katham rāmeṇa vinā nṛpas vasati

कथम् रामेण विना नृपस् वसति ।

(कथं रामेण विना नृपो वसति ।)

f. **rāmas nṛpas bhavati**
rāmas nṛpas bhavati

रामस् नृपस् भवति ।

(रामो नृपो भवति ।)

g. **nṛpas rāmas bhavati**
nṛpas rāmas bhavati

नृपस् रामस् भवति ।

(नृपो रामो भवति ।)

h. **vīras amṛtānām grāme vasati**
vīras amṛtānām grāme vasati

वीरस् अमृतानाम् ग्रामे वसति ।

(वीरो ऽमृतानां ग्रामे वसति ।)

7. a. How can the men see the king without the sun?

b. The students' teacher reads the book.

LESSON EIGHT (CONTINUED)

c. "Here in the forest is fruit," the boy says to the hero.

d. The deer lives in the forest and the elephant lives in the village.

e. "Knowledge is not in the book," the teacher says.

f. Without the book the student remembers the knowledge.

g. "Rāma, where are you going with the deer?" the son asks.

h. The king reads the book to the boy.

8. a. **kutra amṛtasya jñānam paṭhasi**
kutrāmṛtasya jñānam paṭhasi (with vowel **sandhi**)

कुत्रामृतस्य ज्ञानम् पठसि । (with vowel **sandhi**)

(कुत्रामृतस्य ज्ञानं पठसि ।) (with complete **sandhi**)

b. **katham aśvais vinā rāmas vanam gacchati**
katham aśvais vinā rāmas vanam gacchati

कथम् अश्वैस् विना रामस् वनम् गच्छति ।

(कथमश्वैर्विना रामो वनं गच्छति ।)

c. **pustake sūktāni bhavanti iti ācāryas śiṣyān vadati**
pustake sūktāni bhavantīty ācāryas śiṣyān vadati

पुस्तके सूक्तानि भवन्तीत्याचार्यस् शिष्यान् वदति ।

(पुस्तके सूक्तानि भवन्तीत्याचार्यः शिष्यान्वदति ।)

LESSON EIGHT (CONTINUED)

d. rāmas satyam paśyati satyam vadati ca
rāmas satyam paśyati satyam vadati ca

रामस् सत्यम् पश्यति सत्यम् वदति च ।

(रामः सत्यं पश्यति सत्यं वदति च ।)

e. sūryam candram ca paśyāmi iti nṛpasya putras vadati
sūryam candram ca paśyāmīti nṛpasya putras vadati

सूर्यम् चन्द्रम् च पश्यामीति नृपस्य पुत्रस् वदति ।

(सूर्यं चन्द्रं च पश्यामीति नृपस्य पुत्रो वदति ।)

f. jñānena vinā tatra ācāryās śiṣyās vā na bhavanti
jñānena vinā tatrācāryās śiṣyās vā na bhavanti

ज्ञानेन विना तत्राचार्यास् शिष्यास् वा न भवन्ति ।

(ज्ञानेन विना तत्राचार्याः शिष्या वा न भवन्ति ।)

g. vīras amṛtam bālān vadati
vīras amṛtam bālān vadati

वीरस् अमृतम् बालान् वदति ।

(वीरो ऽमृतं बालान्वदति ।)

LESSON EIGHT (CONTINUED)

h. **grāmāt aśvās gajās bālās ca āgacchanti**
grāmāt aśvās gajās bālās cāgacchanti

ग्रामात् अश्वास् गजास् बालास् चागच्छन्ति ।

(ग्रामादश्वा गजा बालाश्चागच्छन्ति ।)

9.
1. **purāṇa** (ancient)
2. **rāma** (Rāma, hero of the *Rāmāyaṇa*)
3. **puruṣa** (man, or consciousness)
4. **prakṛti** (nature)
5. **prajñā** (intellect)
6. **sītā** (Sītā, Rāma's wife)
7. **sukham** (happiness)
8. **saṃyama** (last three of the eight limbs of yoga)
9. **saṃsāra** (creation)
10. **saṃskāra** (impression)
11. **saṃskṛta** (perfected, put together)
12. **satyam** (truth)
13. **rāma-rājya** (kingdom of Rāma)
14. **rāmāyaṇa** (life of Rāma)
15. **śiṣya** (student)
16. **sthita-prajña** (established in wisdom)
17. **bhagavad-gītā** (Song of the Lord)
18. **samādhi** (even intellect)
19. **śaṅkara** (Shankara)
20. **buddha** (Buddha)
21. **mahābhārata** (Great India)
22. **prajñāparādha** (mistake of the intellect)
23. **vedānta** (culmination of the Veda)
24. **veda-līlā** (play of knowledge)

THE MONKEY AND THE CROCODILE

1. **tatra gaṅgāyām kumbhīras bhavati**
   (tatra gaṅgāyāṃ kumbhīro bhavati)
2. **vānaras taṭe vasati**
   (vānaras taṭe vasati)
3. **vānaras phalāni kumbhīrāya nikṣipati**
   (vānaraḥ phalāni kumbhīrāya nikṣipati)
4. **kumbhīras phalāni khādati**
   (kumbhīraḥ phalāni khādati)
5. **bhāryā vānarasya hṛdayam icchati**
   (bhāryā vānarasya hṛdayam icchati)
6. **hṛdayam vṛkṣe bhavatīti vānaras vadati**
   (hṛdayaṃ vṛkṣe bhavatīti vānaro vadati)
7. **kaścit hṛdayam corayatīti vānaras vadati**
   (kaścid dhṛdayaṃ corayatīti vānaro vadati)
8. **evam kumbhīras vānaras ca mitre tiṣṭhataḥ**
   (evaṃ kumbhīro vānaraś ca mitre tiṣṭhataḥ)

1. There is a crocodile in the Ganges.
2. A monkey lives on the bank (of the river).
3. The monkey throws down fruit for the crocodile.
4. The crocodile eats the fruit.
5. The wife wants (to eat) the monkey's heart.

6. "The heart is in the tree!" the monkey says.

7. "Someone steals the heart," the monkey says.

8. Therefore, the crocodile and the monkey remain friends (stand in friendship).

LESSON NINE

1. a. रामो गच्छति
   b. बाला आगच्छन्ति
   c. वीरावागच्छतः
   d. शिष्यो ऽत्र
   e. राम इति
   f. देवाः स्मरन्ति
   g. पुत्रः पश्यति
   h. अश्वो वदति

2. a. रामस् गच्छति
   b. कुत्र आगच्छसि
   c. सूर्यस् चन्द्रस् च
   d. गजैस् वीरस्
   e. अश्वास् आगच्छन्ति
   f. रामस् पुत्रस् च
   g. गजैस् सह
   h. फलयोस् जलम्

3. a. The hero has a boy. (Of the hero a boy is.)
   b. Happiness is the fruit of knowledge.
   c. The students obtain water from the house for the teacher.
   d. "Rāma goes there for the water," the hero says.
   e. The student serves the teacher.
   f. The students obtain knowledge from the teacher.
   g. Oh Rāma! How do you conquer suffering?

LESSON NINE (CONTINUED)

h. The son goes from the house on the king's horses.

i. "Immortality is the fruit of happiness," he thinks.

j. The teacher reads the book of knowledge to the student.

4. a. जलम् रामस्य हस्तयोस् भवति । (without **sandhi**)

   जलम् रामस्य हस्तयोर्भवति । (with vowel and final **s** **sandhi**)

   (जलं रामस्य हस्तयोर्भवति ।) (with complete **sandhi**)

   b. बालस् पुस्तकम् पठति ।

   बालः पुस्तकम् पठति ।

   (बालः पुस्तकं पठति ।)

   c. वीरस् नृपस्य गृहे एव तिष्ठति ।

   वीरो नृपस्य गृह एव तिष्ठति ।

   (वीरो नृपस्य गृह एव तिष्ठति ।)

LESSON NINE

(CONTINUED)

d. बालास् वनात् फलानि लभन्ते ।

बाला वनात् फलानि लभन्ते ।

(बाला वनात्फलानि लभन्ते ।)

e. ज्ञानेन दुःखम् जयसि इति आचार्यस् वदति ।

ज्ञानेन दुःखम् जयसीत्याचार्यो वदति ।

(ज्ञानेन दुःखं जयसीत्याचार्यो वदति ।)

f. फलात् बालस् जलम् लभते ।

फलात् बालो जलम् लभते ।

(फलाद्बालो जलं लभते ।)

g. सूर्ये चन्द्रे च सत्यम् पश्यामि इति रामस् वदति ।

सूर्ये चन्द्रे च सत्यम् पश्यामीति रामो वदति ।

(सूर्ये चन्द्रे च सत्यं पश्यामीति रामो वदति ।)

LESSON NINE

(CONTINUED)

h. ज्ञानेन विना दुःखम् भवति ।

ज्ञानेन विना दुःखम् भवति ।

(ज्ञानेन विना दुःखं भवति ।)

i. ग्रामात् न आगच्छामि इति नृपस्य पुत्रस् वदति ।

ग्रामात् नागच्छामीति नृपस्य पुत्रो वदति ।

(ग्रामान्नागच्छामीति नृपस्य पुत्रो वदति ।)

j. वीरस् बालस् च वने वसतः ।

वीरो बालश्च वने वसतः ।

(वीरो बालश्च वने वसतः ।)

THE RĀMĀYAṆA

1. **ayodhyāyām daśaratho nāma nṛpo vasati**
   (ayodhyāyāṃ daśaratho nāma nṛpo vasati)
2. **daśarathasya catvāraḥ putrā bhavanti**
   (daśarathasya catvāraḥ putrā bhavanti)
3. **putrā rāmo bharato lakṣmaṇaḥ śatrughno bhavanti**
   (putrā rāmo bharato lakṣmaṇaḥ śatrughno bhavanti)
4. **rāmaḥ sundaraḥ śānto vīraś ca bhavati**
   (rāmaḥ sundaraḥ śānto vīraś ca bhavati)
5. **nṛpo rāme snihyati**
   (nṛpo rāme snihyati)
6. **rāmo mithilām lakṣmaṇena saha gacchati**
   (rāmo mithilāṃ lakṣmaṇena saha gacchati)
7. **tatra rāmaḥ sītām paśyati**
   (tatra rāmaḥ sītāṃ paśyati)
8. **sītāyām snihyāmīti rāmo vadati**
   (sītāyāṃ snihyāmīti rāmo vadati)

1. In Ayodhyā lives a king named Daśaratha.
2. Daśaratha has four sons.
3. The sons are Rāma, Bharata, Lakṣmaṇa, and Śatrughna.
4. Rāma is beautiful, peaceful, and strong.
5. The king loves Rāma.
6. Rāma goes to Mithilā with Lakṣmaṇa.
7. There Rāma sees Sītā.
8. "I love Sītā," Rāma says.

LESSON TEN

1\. a. मम पुत्रो गच्छति ।

My son goes.

b. तव गजो मत्त्वां गच्छति ।

Your elephant goes from me to you.

c. मम हस्तौ पुस्तकेषु स्तः ।

My hands are on the books.

d. अहं नृपो ऽस्मि ।

I am the king.

e. वयमश्वे तिष्ठामः ।

We are standing on the horse.

f. त्वं मम पुस्तकं पठसि ।

You are reading my book.

g. रामस्तव नृपो ऽस्ति ।

Rāma is your king.

h. यूयं गृहे स्थ ।

You are all in the house.

i. अस्माकं नृपः कुपितो ऽस्ति ।

Our king is angry.

j. त्वया सहाहं गच्छामि ।

I am going with you.

k. धार्मिकस्य नृपस्य भीतो ऽस्ति ।

The virtuous king has fear. (Of the virtuous king fear is.)

LESSON TEN
(CONTINUED)

1. त्वं सुन्दरः ।

   You are beautiful.

2. a. The king has a son.

   b. Aha! Rāma is speaking again.

   c. I am very afraid.

   d. Even teachers read books.

   e. There is a king named Rāma in the forest.

   f. "How do I go to your house?" the student asks.

   g. The hero conquers my village.

   h. The son obtains water from the beautiful fruit.

   i. Without happiness there is suffering.

   j. The son thinks that the elephant is beautiful.

3. a. शिष्यस् आचार्यात् भीतस् न अस्ति ।

   शिष्य आचार्याद्भीतो नास्ति ।

LESSON TEN

(CONTINUED)

b. त्वम् शास्त्रेभ्यस् ज्ञानम् लभसे ।

त्वं शास्त्रेभ्यो ज्ञानं लभसे ।

c. तत्र बालस् अस्ति इति वीरस् आचार्यम् वदति ।

तत्र बालो ऽस्तीति वीर आचार्यं वदति ।

d. अहम् मृगम् आचार्यम् पृच्छामि ।

अहं मृगमाचार्यं पृच्छामि ।

e. कुत्र गच्छसि इति बालस् पृच्छति ।

कुत्र गच्छसीति बालः पृच्छति ।

f. पुनर् वीरस् मम गृहम् आगच्छति ।

पुनर्वीरो मम गृहमागच्छति ।

g. तव आचार्यस् सत्यम् वदति ।

तवाचार्यः सत्यं वदति ।

LESSON TEN

(CONTINUED)

h. अस्माकम् अश्वास् ग्रामे तिष्ठन्ति ।

अस्माकमश्वा ग्रामे तिष्ठन्ति ।

i. अस्ति नृपस् रामस् नाम अस्माकम् ग्रामे ।

अस्ति नृपो रामो नामास्माकं ग्रामे ।

j. कथम् त्वत् नृपस्य अश्वान् लभे ।

कथं त्वन्नृपस्याश्वांल्लभे ।

LESSON ELEVEN

1.
a. रामेण सह — with Rāma
b. शास्त्राणि — the scriptures
c. फले अश्वे स्तः । — The two fruits are on the horse. (The dual ends in a **pragṛhya** vowel. See page 91. Otherwise, the following **a** would be dropped.)
d. स गच्छति । — He goes.
e. स बाल आगच्छति । — That boy comes.
f. बालो मामागच्छति । — The boy comes to me.
g. सा बाला मामागच्छति । — That girl comes to me.
h. तां गच्छति । — He goes to her.
i. स बालो गच्छति । — That boy goes.
j. सा बाला गच्छति । — That girl goes.
k. स बाल इव गच्छामि । — Like that boy, I go.
l. अहो राम — Hey Rāma!
m. तस्मिन्वने स वसति । — He lives in that forest.
n. सीताया माला — Sītā's garland

LESSON ELEVEN (CONTINUED)

2. a. That army conquers the king.
   b. Like Rāma, the boy is virtuous.
   c. Your child reads the story.
   d. The children stand in the shadow of the elephant.
   e. Sītā is the daughter of the king.
   f. He serves the teacher's wife.
   g. The king has a daughter.
   h. With knowledge the student obtains immortality.
   i. Like that girl, she goes to the house.

3. a. अस्ति कन्या सीता नाम तस्मिन् ग्रामे ।

   अस्ति कन्या सीता नाम तस्मिन्ग्रामे ।

   b. धार्मिकस्य नृपस्य पुत्रिका अतीव भीता ।

   धार्मिकस्य नृपस्य पुत्रिकातीव भीता ।

   c. पुनर् माम् वदति इति सा प्रजा वदति ।

   पुनर्मां वदतीति सा प्रजा वदति ।

LESSON ELEVEN

(CONTINUED)

d. अहो अहम् ताम् कथाम् स्मरे इति कन्या वदति ।

अहो अहं तां कथां स्मर इति कन्या वदति ।

Using the middle ending for remember gives a more reflexive sense to the word "remember."

e. विद्यया अमृतम् लभसे । अविद्यया दुःखम् लभसे ।

विद्ययामृतं लभसे । अविद्यया दुःखं लभसे ।

f. तास् कन्यास् इव सीता पुस्तकानि पठति ।

ताः कन्या इव सीता पुस्तकानि पठति ।

g. कुत्र आवयोस् पुत्रिका अस्ति इति वीरस् भार्याम् पृच्छति । ("Our" is dual.)

कुत्रावयोः पुत्रिकास्तीति वीरो भार्यां पृच्छति ।

h. रामस्य भार्या सीता अस्ति ।

रामस्य भार्या सीतास्ति ।

LESSON ELEVEN

(CONTINUED)

i. वीरस् मालाम् लभते एवम् च भार्याम् लभते ।

वीरो मालां लभत एवं च भार्यां लभते ।

j. सीतया विना सूर्येन विना इव अस्मि इति रामस् वदति ।

सीतया विना सूर्येण विनेवास्मीति रामो वदति ।

THE MONKEY AND THE CROCODILE

4. a. There is in the Ganges a crocodile.
   b. His friend, a monkey, lives on the bank of the Ganges.
   c. Everyday the monkey throws down ripe fruits.
   d. The crocodile eats the fruits.
   e. "The heart of the monkey is sweet!" says the wife of the crocodile.
   f. The wife wants to eat the heart.
   g. "Hey monkey! Come to my house!" the crocodile says to the monkey.
   h. "OK" the monkey says.
   i. The crocodile carries the monkey on his back.
   j. In the middle of the Ganges the crocodile tells the truth.
   k. "My heart is in the tree!" the monkey says.
   l. "Take me there again," the monkey says.
   m. The crock takes the monkey to the bank of the river.
   n. The monkey jumps up to the tree.
   o. The monkey looks in the hole of the tree.
   p. "Someone has stolen my heart!" the monkey says.
   q. Therefore the crocodile and the monkey remain friends.

LESSON TWELVE

1. a. Having seen the fire, the horse goes from the house.
   b. The student lives in the village.
   c. The seers see the hymns of the scriptures.
   d. The king serves the tenth guest.
   e. Having conquered the village, the hero obtains fame.
   f. The siddha lives in the village.
   g. "Hey Rāma! Where are you going?" the second hero asks.
   h. Having read the book, the poet thinks about it.
   i. With truth comes peace.
   j. "We live on the earth," the people say.

2. a. सेनाम् जित्वा वीरस् भूमौ कीर्तिम् लभते ।१।
   सेनां जित्वा वीरो भूमौ कीर्तिं लभते ।१।

   b. सीता रामस् च इव शिष्यस् वनम् गच्छति ।२।
   सीता रामश्चेव शिष्यो वनं गच्छति ।२।

   c. तृतीयम् तस्यास् अतिथिम् सेवित्वा सीता रामम् वदति ।३।

LESSON TWELVE

(CONTINUED)

तृतीयं तस्या अतिथिं सेवित्वा सीता रामं वदति ।३।

d. कथायाम् रामस् कीर्तिम् लभते ।४।

कथायां रामः कीर्तिं लभते ।४।

e. वीरस् अविद्याम् न जयते ।५।

वीरो ऽविद्यां न जयते ।५।

f. नृपस् रामस् नाम अतीव धार्मिकस् अस्ति ।६।

नृपो रामो नामातीव धार्मिको ऽस्ति ।६।

g. कथम् सिद्धिम् लभसे इति द्वितीयस् शिष्यस् पृच्छति ।७।

कथं सिद्धिं लभस इति द्वितीयः शिष्यः पृच्छति ।७।

LESSON TWELVE

(CONTINUED)

h. तस्य भार्यया सह वने उषित्वा नृपस् रामस् नाम
ग्रामम् गच्छति ।८।
तस्य भार्यया सह वन उषित्वा नृपो रामो नाम
ग्रामं गच्छति ।८।

i. शान्तिम् सिद्धिम् कीर्तिम् च लब्ध्वा ऋषिस्
सुन्दरम् वनम् गच्छति ।९।
शान्तिं सिद्धिं कीर्तिं च लब्ध्वर्षिः सुन्दरं
वनं गच्छति ।९।

j. गजे एवम् तस्य भार्याम् दृष्ट्वा वीरस् ताम्
गच्छति ।१०।
गज एवं तस्य भार्यां दृष्ट्वा वीरस्तां
गच्छति ।१०।

LESSON THIRTEEN

1. a. Where there is peace, there is perfection.
   b. The girl who is my wife's daughter lives here.
   c. "Sītā is the beautiful daughter of the king," Rāma says.
   d. Since the horses are not coming here, the men and the boys are going there.
   e. Having gone to the river, the two friends read books.
   f. When the army serves the king, then the virtuous king conquers.
   g. If a man obtains perfection, then he becomes a sage.
   h. The poet reads the story to the boy who is his guest.
   i. With the friend, the man goes to the beautiful river.
   j. The hero remembers the village from which I come.

2. a. नद्यास् जलम् बालस् लभते ।१।

   नद्या जलं बालो लभते ।१।

   b. यत् वाप्याम् अस्ति तत् फलम् पत्नी पश्यति ।२।

   यद्वाप्यामस्ति तत्फलं पत्नी पश्यति ।२।

   c. मालाम् लब्ध्वा अस्माकम् अतिथिस् ग्रामम् गच्छति ।३।

   मालां लब्ध्वास्माकमतिथिर्ग्रामं गच्छति ।३।

LESSON THIRTEEN

(CONTINUED)

d. यदा तस्य पत्नी तम् सेवते तदा सस् नृपस् इव वसति ।४।

यदा तस्य पत्नी तं सेवते तदा स नृप इव वसति ।४।

e. या रामस्य भार्या भवति सा सीता भूमौ कीर्तिम् लभते ।५।

या रामस्य भार्या भवति सा सीता भूमौ कीर्तिं लभते ।५।

f. यस् बालस् आगच्छति तम् धार्मिकस् नृपस् पश्यति ।६।

यो बाल आगच्छति तं धार्मिको नृपः पश्यति ।६।

g. शिष्यस् मत्वा नदीम् कविम् पृच्छति ।७।

शिष्यो मत्वा नदीं कविं पृच्छति ।७।

h. सा सुन्दरी पत्नी दुःखेन विना वसति ।८।

सा सुन्दरी पत्नी दुःखेन विना वसति ।८।

i. यस् नरस् पश्यति तस्मै अविद्या छाया इव भवति ।९।

LESSON THIRTEEN (CONTINUED)

यो नरः पश्यति तस्मा अविद्या छायेव
भवति ।९।

j. यदा नृपस्य पुत्रिका आगच्छति तदा प्रजास्
तिष्ठन्ति ।१०।

यदा नृपस्य पुत्रिकागच्छति तदा प्रजास्तिष्ठन्ति ।१०।

LESSON FOURTEEN

3. a. When the student brings water, then the teacher drinks it.
   b. The boy led the elephants to the pond. (A double accusative is a common formation in Sanskrit.)
   c. The poet speaks to the man who is approaching the village.
   d. Rāma said that the hero protects the village from the angry king.
   e. Seeing the elephant in the pond, the seer laughed and laughed.
   f. "I know your beautiful wife," the girl said to the hero.
   g. The wife returned to the house in which she lived.
   h. The sage knows peace, truth, perfection, immortality, and happiness.
   i. The hero protected the village from the army.
   j. Having seen the beautiful king, the boy laughed.

4. a. कविस् पुस्तकम् अपठत् जलम् अपिबत् इव ।१।

   कविः पुस्तकमपठज्जलमपिबदिव ।१।

   b. कथम् सेनायास् ग्रामम् गोपयामि इति वीरस् अपृच्छत् ।२।

   कथं सेनाया ग्रामं गोपयामीति वीरो ऽपृच्छत् ।२।

   c. कथम् ऋषयस् अग्निना विना अवसन् ।३।

LESSON FOURTEEN

(CONTINUED)

कथमृषयो ऽग्निना विनावसन् ।३।

d. यदि अश्वास् नदीम् प्रतिगच्छन्ति तदा बालस् तान् वनम् नयति ।४।

यद्यश्वा नदीं प्रतिगच्छन्ति तदा बालस्तान्वनं नयति ।४।

e. यदा नरस् दुःखम् न बोधति तदा सिद्धिम् उपगच्छति ।५।

यदा नरो दुःखं न बोधति तदा सिद्धिमुपगच्छति ।५।

f. नृपस् रामस् नाम तस्य भार्यायै सीतायै मालाम् आनयत् ।६।

नृपो रामो नाम तस्य भार्यायै सीतायै मालामानयत् ।६।

g. नरस् अविद्याम् विद्यया जयति ।७।

नरो ऽविद्यां विद्यया जयति ।७।

h. यत् जलम् नद्यास् आगच्छत् तत् प्रजा अपिबत् ।८।

यज्जलं नद्या आगच्छत्तत्प्रजापिबत् ।८।

LESSON FOURTEEN

(CONTINUED)

i. कन्या नदीम् दृष्ट्वा तस्यास् गृहम् प्रत्यगच्छत् ।९।

कन्या नदीं दृष्ट्वा तस्या गृहं प्रत्यगच्छत् ।९।

j. बालस् वनात् नदीम् अश्वान् अनयत् ।१०।

बालो वनान्नदीमश्वानानयत् ।१०।

LESSON FIFTEEN

3. a. Having understood the story, the poet smiled.
   b. Rāma and Sītā enjoyed the water in the river.
   c When the guest approaches, then the boys stand up.
   d. When the guest approached, then the boys stood up.
   e. Where there is peace, there is happiness.
   f. A daughter is born in the house of the king.
   g. Having conquered ignorance with knowledge, the sage shines like the sun.
   h. "Hey Rāma! How do you stand up on that elephant?" the boy asked.
   i. Having enjoyed the fruit in the forest, the wife of the hero returned to the house.
   j. Rāma smiled at the boy who is his son.

4. Sentences will be given with **sandhi**. If the **sandhi** is difficult, the sentence will be given without **sandhi** first.
   a. यथातिथिः फलमरमत तथा गृहं पुनः प्रतिगच्छति ।१।
   b. स्मित्वा सीता सुन्दरीं बालामवदत् ।२।
   c. गजादागत्य स तं ग्राममुपागच्छत् ।३।
   d. नरस्य पुत्रो ऽस्तीत्यवगच्छति ।४।
   e. फलाज्जलं पीत्वा कन्योत्तिष्ठति ।५।

LESSON FIFTEEN (CONTINUED)

f. यदा चन्द्रः शोभते तदा वने छायाः पश्यसि ।६।

g. यदा बालो गजं पश्यति तदा स्मयते हसति च ।७।

h. नरस्तस्य पत्नी च तत्सुन्दरं गृहं रमेते ।८।

i. यदा तस्य पुत्रस् उदभवत् तदा वीरस् अस्मयत ।९।

यदा तस्य पुत्र उदभवत्तदा वीरो ऽस्मयत ।९।

j. यस् नरस् तिष्ठति तस्मात् कन्या फलानि अलभत ।१०।

यो नरस्तिष्ठति तस्मात्कन्या फलान्यलभत ।१०।

LESSON SIXTEEN

5. a. Kṛṣṇa protected the horses, deer, and elephants. (This could be written in other ways, such as "horse, deer, and elephant.")
   b. The beloved king, Rāma, smiled to the boys of the village.
   c. The girl protected the child from the sun with her shadow.
   d. He who knows the Self, (he) enjoys action. ("Action" is sometimes put in the plural when it is used in this way.)
   e. The child laughed at the black horse's action.
   f. The boy stood up when she said his name.
   g. Having approached his dear son, the hero smiled.
   h. The boy and girl are the children of the shining king.
   i. The white horses were in the forest.
   j. In the village there was a king, named Rāma.

6. a. कृष्णाश्वो नद्या जलं पिबति ।१।
   b. य आत्मानं बोधति स कर्माकर्म रमते ।२।
   c. राज्ञो नाम कृष्ण आसीत् ।३।
   d. राजा पुत्रस्य रमणीयानि कर्माणि रमते ।४।
   e. प्रियस् वीरस् सिद्धि असिद्धिम् अवागच्छत् ।५।
   प्रियो वीरः सिद्ध्यसिद्धिमवागच्छत् ।५।
   f. बालो गजादागच्छति गृहं प्रतिगच्छति च ।६।

LESSON SIXTEEN

(CONTINUED)

g. यो नागच्छति न गच्छति स आत्मा ।७।

h. यदा राजोपागच्छत्तदा बालबाला उदतिष्ठन् ।८।

i. यस् नरस् राजा आसीत् सस् कृष्णात् वनात्

आगच्छत् ।९।

यो नरो राजासीत्स कृष्णाद्वनादागच्छत् ।९।

j. आत्मनस् ज्ञानम् सूर्यचन्द्रयोस् ज्ञानम् अपि

अस्ति ।१०।

आत्मनो ज्ञानं सूर्यचन्द्रयोर्ज्ञानमप्यस्ति ।१०।

LESSON SEVENTEEN 4.

a. "My father will go there," the boy said to his mother.

b. "When will your brother obtain the water?" the father asked.

c. The father and mother will protect the family from the water.

d. "When will you come from the forest?" Rāma asked his brother.

e. After serving his father, Rāma will be the king.

f. She smiles when she thinks of her brother.

g. A mother is the giver of happiness to her child.

h. He who conquers the Self is a maker of peace.

i. After drinking the water, he will read his mother's book.

h. Rāma will live in the forest with the brother.

5. a. यदा मम स्वसा उद्भवत् तदा सा मम
मातरम् अस्मयत ।१।
यदा मम स्वसोद्भवत्तदा सा मम
मातरमस्मयत ।१।

b. मम कुलस्य नाम ऋषेस् नाम्नस् भवति ।२।
मम कुलस्य नामर्षेर्नाम्नो भवति ।२।

c. कदा राजानं वदिष्यामीति तस्याः
पितामन्यत ।३।

LESSON SEVENTEEN (CONTINUED)

d. तस्याः पितुः पत्नी तस्या माता भवति ।४।

e. मम पितास्माकं कुले शान्तेः कर्तास्ति ।५।

f. भ्रातास्वसारौ वनात्फलानि लप्स्येते ।६।

g. वीरस् वने अग्नेस् राजानम् गोपयिष्यति ।७।

वीरो वने ऽग्ने राजानं गोपयिष्यति ।७।

h. राज्ञः पुत्रस्य भ्रातरो न भवन्ति ।८।

i. कदा शिष्यास् धार्मिकात् आचार्यात् ज्ञानम् लप्स्यन्ते ।९।

कदा शिष्या धार्मिकादाचार्याज्ज्ञानं लप्स्यन्ते ।९।

j. वाप्याम् त्वाम् अपश्यम् इति राजा सुन्दरम् पुत्रम् वदति ।१०।

वाप्यां त्वामपश्यमिति राजा सुन्दरं पुत्रं वदति ।१०।

LESSON EIGHTEEN

4. a. The white cow stands in the pond and drinks water.
   b. The sage has conquered the enemy.
   c. If the forest is full of fruit, then the cows go there.
   d. My mother reads the little book and enjoys it.
   e. A teacher is the giver of much happiness.
   f. The little boy shines like the white sun.
   g. When you understand the Self, then you are the cause of much happiness.
   h. When will the pleasant king protect our family from the enemy?
   i. The swift girl comes from the forest with fruit.
   j. The cause of the teacher's happiness is the attainments of his students.

5. a. सुन्दराल्पधेनुर्वाप्या जलमपिबत् ।१।
   b. शीघ्रकृष्णाश्वो ऽल्पे ग्रामे तिष्ठति ।२।
   c. शत्रुं जित्वा सेना शान्तिसुखे रंस्यते ।३।
   d. अविद्या सत्यशत्रुः ।४।
   e. आत्मानं बुद्ध्वा स कर्माकर्मस्य
   हेतुमवागच्छत् ।५।

LESSON EIGHTEEN

(CONTINUED)

f. प्रजा सुन्दरे वने ऽल्पगृह उद्भवत् ।६।

g. शिष्यस्तस्य गुरवे सुन्दरमालामानेष्यति ।७।

h. वनं फलपूर्णं भवति वापी च जलपूर्णा भवति ।८।

i. तस्य कुलं दृष्ट्वा पिता जलाय वनमगच्छत् ।९।

j. कदा सुन्दरी धेनुरत्र शिघ्रनद्या
आगमिष्यति ।१०।

a
MASCULINE

Stem: **nara** (masculine) man

	Singular	Dual	Plural
Nominative	नरस् **naras**	नरौ **narau**	नरास् **narās**
Accusative	नरम् **naram**	नरौ **narau**	नरान् **narān**
Instrumental	नरेण **nareṇa***	नराभ्याम् **narābhyām**	नरैस् **narais**
Dative	नराय **narāya**	नराभ्याम् **narābhyām**	नरेभ्यस् **narebhyas**
Ablative	नरात् **narāt**	नराभ्याम् **narābhyām**	नरेभ्यस् **narebhyas**
Genitive	नरस्य **narasya**	नरयोस् **narayos**	नराणाम् **narāṇām***
Locative	नरे **nare**	नरयोस् **narayos**	नरेषु **nareṣu**
Vocative	नर **nara**	नरौ **narau**	नरास् **narās**

*The instrumental singular for **gaja** is **gajena**, and the genitive plural for **gaja** is **gajānām**. The **r** in **nareṇa** and **narāṇām** causes the **n** to become **ṇ**. (See page 142, 143.)

a
NEUTER

Stem: **phala** (neuter) fruit

	Singular	Dual	Plural
Nominative	फलम् **phalam**	फले **phale**	फलानि **phalāni**
Accusative	फलम् **phalam**	फले **phale**	फलानि **phalāni**
Instrumental	फलेन **phalena**	फलाभ्याम् **phalābhyām**	फलैस् **phalais**
Dative	फलाय **phalāya**	फलाभ्याम् **phalābhyām**	फलेभ्यस् **phalebhyas**
Ablative	फलात् **phalāt**	फलाभ्याम् **phalābhyām**	फलेभ्यस् **phalebhyas**
Genitive	फलस्य **phalasya**	फलयोस् **phalayos**	फलानाम् **phalānām**
Locative	फले **phale**	फलयोस् **phalayos**	फलेषु **phaleṣu**
Vocative	फल **phala**	फले **phale**	फलानि **phalāni**

ā

FEMININE

Stem: **mālā** (feminine) garland

	Singular	Dual	Plural
Nom	माला **mālā**	माले **māle**	मालास् **mālās**
Acc	मालाम् **mālām**	माले **māle**	मालास् **mālās**
Inst	मालया **mālayā**	मालाभ्याम् **mālābhyām**	मालाभिस् **mālābhis**
Dat	मालायै **mālāyai**	मालाभ्याम् **mālābhyām**	मालाभ्यस् **mālābhyas**
Abl	मालायास् **mālāyās**	मालाभ्याम् **mālābhyām**	मालाभ्यस् **mālābhyas**
Gen	मालायास् **mālāyās**	मालयोस् **mālayos**	मालानाम् **mālānām**
Loc	मालायाम् **mālāyām**	मालयोस् **mālayos**	मालासु **mālāsu**
Voc	माले **māle**	माले **māle**	मालास् **mālās**

i
MASCULINE FEMININE

Stem: **agni** (masculine) fire; **kīrti** (feminine) glory

Nom	अग्निस् agnis	अग्नी agnī	अग्नयस् agnayas
Acc	अग्निम् agnim	अग्नी agnī	अग्नीन् कीर्तीस् agnīn / kīrtīs
Inst	अग्निना कीर्त्या agninā / kīrtyā	अग्निभ्याम् agnibhyām	अग्निभिस् agnibhis
Dat	अग्नये कीर्त्यै agnaye (kīrtyai)	अग्निभ्याम् agnibhyām	अग्निभ्यस् agnibhyas
Abl	अग्नेस् कीर्त्यास् agnes (kīrtyās)	अग्निभ्याम् agnibhyām	अग्निभ्यस् agnibhyas
Gen	अग्नेस् कीर्त्यास् agnes (kīrtyās)	अग्न्योस् agnyos	अग्नीनाम् agnīnām
Loc	अग्नौ कीर्त्याम् agnau (kīrtyām)	अग्न्योस् agnyos	अग्निषु agniṣu
Voc	अग्ने agne	अग्नी agnī	अग्नयस् agnayas

The singular dative, ablative, genitive, and locative have an optional feminine form. For example,the feminine dative singular is **kīrtaye** or **kīrtyai**. The feminine instrumental singular is **kīrtyā**.

ī

FEMININE

Stem: **vāpī** (feminine) pond

	Singular	Dual	Plural
Nom	वापी vāpī	वाप्यौ vāpyau	वाप्यस् vāpyas
Acc	वापीम् vāpīm	वाप्यौ vāpyau	वापीस् vāpīs
Inst	वाप्या vāpyā	वापीभ्याम् vāpībhyām	वापीभिस् vāpībhis
Dat	वाप्यै vāpyai	वापीभ्याम् vāpībhyām	वापीभ्यस् vāpībhyas
Abl	वाप्यास् vāpyās	वापीभ्याम् vāpībhyām	वापीभ्यस् vāpībhyas
Gen	वाप्यास् vāpyās	वाप्योस् vāpyos	वापीनाम् vāpīnām
Loc	वाप्याम् vāpyām	वाप्योस् vāpyos	वापीषु vāpīṣu
Voc	वापि vāpi	वाप्यौ vāpyau	वाप्यस् vāpyas

an

MASCULINE

Stem: **rājan** (masculine) king; **ātman** (masculine) Self

	Singular	Dual	Plural
Nom	राजा **rājā**	राजानौ **rājānau**	राजानस् **rājānas**
Acc	राजानम् **rājānam**	राजानौ **rājānau**	राज्ञस् आत्मनस् **rājñas/ātmanas**
Inst	राज्ञ आत्मना **rājñā/ātmanā**	राजभ्याम् **rājabhyām**	राजभिस् **rājabhis**
Dat	राज्ञे आत्मने **rājñe/ātmane**	राजभ्याम् **rājabhyām**	राजभ्यस् **rājabhyas**
Abl	राज्ञस् आत्मनस् **rājñas/ātmanas**	राजभ्याम् **rājabhyām**	राजभ्यस् **rājabhyas**
Gen	राज्ञस् आत्मनस् **rājñas/ātmanas**	राज्ञोस् आत्मनोस् **rājños/ātmanos**	राज्ञाम् आत्मनाम् **rājñām/ātmanām**
Loc	राज्ञि आत्मनि **rājni/ātmani**	राज्ञोस् आत्मनोस् **rājños/ātmanos**	राजसु **rājasu**
Voc	राजन् **rājan**	राजानौ **rājānau**	राजानस् **rājānas**

an

NEUTER

Stem: **nāman** (neuter) name

	Singular	Dual	Plural
Nom	नाम nāma	नाम्नी नामनी nāmnī/nāmanī	नामानि nāmāni
Acc	नाम nāma	नाम्नी नामनी nāmnī/nāmanī	नामानि nāmāni
Inst	नाम्ना nāmnā	नामभ्याम् nāmabhyām	नामभिस् nāmabhis
Dat	नाम्ने nāmne	नामभ्याम् nāmabhyām	नामभ्यस् nāmabhyas
Abl	नाम्नस् nāmnas	नामभ्याम् nāmabhyām	नामभ्यस् nāmabhyas
Gen	नाम्नस् nāmnas	नाम्नोस् nāmnos	नाम्नाम् nāmnām
Loc	नाम्नि नामनि nāmni/nāmani	नाम्नोस् nāmnos	नामसु nāmasu
Voc	नामन् नाम nāman/nāma	नाम्नी नामनी nāmnī/nāmanī	नामानि nāmāni

ṛ
MASCULINE
FEMININE

Stem: **dātṛ** (masculine) giver; **svasṛ** (feminine) sister

Nom	दाता **dātā**	दातारौ **dātārau**	दातारस् **dātāras**
Acc	दातारम् **dātāram**	दातारौ **dātārau**	दातॄन् स्वसॄस् **dātṝn / svasṝs**
Inst	दात्रा **dātrā**	दातृभ्याम् **dātṛbhyām**	दातृभिस् **dātṛbhis**
Dat	दात्रे **dātre**	दातृभ्याम् **dātṛbhyām**	दातृभ्यस् **dātṛbhyas**
Abl	दातुस् **dātus**	दातृभ्याम् **dātṛbhyām**	दातृभ्यस् **dātṛbhyas**
Gen	दातुस् **dātus**	दात्रोस् **dātros**	दातॄणाम् **dātṝṇām**
Loc	दातरि **dātari**	दात्रोस् **dātros**	दातृषु **dātṛṣu**
Voc	दातर् **dātar**	दातारौ **dātārau**	दातारस् **dātāras**

Stem: **pitṛ** (mas) father; **mātṛ** (fem) mother; **bhrātṛ** (mas) brother

(These nouns follow **dātṛ** in all other cases.)

Nom	पिता **pitā**	पितरौ **pitarau**	पितरस् **pitaras**
Acc	पितरम् **pitaram**	पितरौ **pitarau**	पितॄन् भ्रातॄन् मातॄस् **pitṝn / bhrātṝn / mātṝs**

u

MASCULINE
FEMININE

Stem: **hetu** (masculine) cause; **dhenu** (feminine) cow

Nom	हेतुस् **hetus**	हेतू **hetū**	हेतवस् **hetavas**
Acc	हेतुम् **hetum**	हेतू **hetū**	हेतून् धेनूस् **hetūn / dhenūs**
Inst	हेतुना धेन्वा **hetunā/dhenvā**	हेतुभ्याम् **hetubhyām**	हेतुभिस् **hetubhis**
Dat	हेतवे धेन्वै **hetave (dhenvai)**	हेतुभ्याम् **hetubhyām**	हेतुभ्यस् **hetubhyas**
Abl	हेतोस् धेन्वास् **hetos (dhenvās)**	हेतुभ्याम् **hetubhyām**	हेतुभ्यस् **hetubhyas**
Gen	हेतोस् धेन्वास् **hetos (dhenvās)**	हेत्वोस् **hetvos**	हेतूनाम् **hetūnām**
Loc	हेतौ धेन्वाम् **hetau (dhenvām)**	हेत्वोस् **hetvos**	हेतुषु **hetuṣu**
Voc	हेतो **heto**	हेतू **hetū**	हेतवस् **hetavas**

The singular dative, ablative, genitive, and locative have an optional feminine form. For example, the feminine dative singular is **dhenave** or **dhenvai**.

mad
asmad

Stem: **mad** (singular) I; **asmad** (plural) we

		Singular	Dual	Plural
I, we	Nom	**अहम्** **aham**	**आवाम्** **āvām**	**वयम्** **vayam**
to me, us	Acc	**माम् मा** **mām** (**mā**)	**आवाम् नौ** **āvām** (**nau**)	**अस्मान् नस्** **asmān** (**nas**)
with me, us	Inst	**मया** **mayā**	**आवाभ्याम्** **āvābhyām**	**अस्माभिस्** **asmābhis**
for me, us	Dat	**मह्यम् मे** **mahyam** (**me**)	**आवाभ्याम् नौ** **āvābhyām** (**nau**)	**अस्मभ्यम् नस्** **asmabhyam** (**nas**)
from me, us	Abl	**मत्** **mat**	**आवाभ्याम्** **āvābhyām**	**अस्मत्** **asmat**
of me, us my, our	Gen	**मम मे** **mama** (**me**)	**आवयोस् नौ** **āvayos** (**nau**)	**अस्माकम् नस्** **asmākam** (**nas**)
on me, us	Loc	**मयि** **mayi**	**आवयोस्** **āvayos**	**अस्मासु** **asmāsu**

tvad
yuṣmad

Stem: **tvad** (singular) you; **yuṣmad** (plural) you

		Singular	Dual	Plural
you	Nom	त्वम् **tvam**	युवाम् **yuvām**	यूयम् **yūyam**
to you	Acc	त्वाम् त्वा **tvām (tvā)**	युवाम् वाम् **yuvām (vām)**	युष्मान् वस् **yuṣmān (vas)**
with you	Inst	त्वया **tvayā**	युवाभ्याम् **yuvābhyām**	युष्माभिस् **yuṣmābhis**
for you	Dat	तुभ्यम् ते **tubhyam (te)**	युवाभ्याम् वाम् **yuvābhyām (vām)**	युष्मभ्यम् वस् **yuṣmabhyam (vas**
from you	Abl	त्वत् **tvat**	युवाभ्याम् **yuvābhyām**	युष्मत् **yuṣmat**
of you your	Gen	तव ते **tava (te)**	युवयोस् वाम् **yuvayos (vām)**	युष्माकम् वस् **yuṣmākam (vas)**
on you	Loc	त्वयि **tvayi**	युवयोस् **yuvayos**	युष्मासु **yuṣmāsu**

tad

MASCULINE

Stem: **tad** (masculine) he

		Singular	Dual	Plural
he, they	Nom	सस् sas	तौ tau	ते te
to him, them	Acc	तम् tam	तौ tau	तान् tān
with him, them	Inst	तेन tena	ताभ्याम् tābhyām	तैस् tais
for him, them	Dat	तस्मै tasmai	ताभ्याम् tābhyām	तेभ्यस् tebhyas
from him, them	Abl	तस्मात् tasmāt	ताभ्याम् tābhyām	तेभ्यस् tebhyas
his, their	Gen	तस्य tasya	तयोस् tayos	तेषाम् teṣām
on him, them	Loc	तस्मिन् tasmin	तयोस् tayos	तेषु teṣu

tad

NEUTER

Stem: **tad** (neuter) it

		Singular	Dual	Plural
it	Nom	तत् **tat**	ते **te**	तानि **tāni**
to it	Acc	तत् **tat**	ते **te**	तानि **tāni**
with it	Inst	तेन **tena**	ताभ्याम् **tābhyām**	तैस् **tais**
for it	Dat	तस्मै **tasmai**	ताभ्याम् **tābhyām**	तेभ्यस् **tebhyas**
from it	Abl	तस्मात् **tasmāt**	ताभ्याम् **tābhyām**	तेभ्यस् **tebhyas**
of it, its	Gen	तस्य **tasya**	तयोस् **tayos**	तेषाम् **teṣām**
on it	Loc	तस्मिन् **tasmin**	तयोस् **tayos**	तेषु **teṣu**

tad

FEMININE

Stem: **tad** (feminine) she

		Singular	Dual	Plural
she	Nom	सा **sā**	ते **te**	तास् **tās**
to her	Acc	ताम् **tām**	ते **te**	तास् **tās**
with her	Inst	तया **tayā**	ताभ्याम् **tābhyām**	ताभिस् **tābhis**
for her	Dat	तस्यै **tasyai**	ताभ्याम् **tābhyām**	ताभ्यस् **tābhyas**
from her	Abl	तस्यास् **tasyās**	ताभ्याम् **tābhyām**	ताभ्यस् **tābhyas**
her	Gen	तस्यास् **tasyās**	तयोस् **tayos**	तासाम् **tāsām**
on her	Loc	तस्याम् **tasyām**	तयोस् **tayos**	तासु **tāsu**

VERBS

ROOT	PRESENT	GERUND	FUTURE	ENGLISH
ava+ √gam	avagacchati	avagatya avagamya	avagamiṣyati	understand
ā+ √gam	āgacchati	āgatya āgamya	āgamiṣyati	come
ā+ √nī	ānayati	ānīya	āneṣyati	bring
ud+√bhū	udbhavati	udbhūya	udbhaviṣyati	born
ud+ √sthā	uttiṣṭhati	utsthāya	utsthāsyati	stand up
upa+ √gam	upagacchati	upagatya upagamya	upagamiṣyati	approach
√gam	gacchati -te	gatvā	gamiṣyati	go
√gup	gopayati -te	gopitvā	gopāyiṣyati	protect
√cint	cintayati -te	cintayitvā	cintayiṣyati	think
√ji	jayati -te	jitvā	jeṣyati	conquer
√dṛś (√paś)	paśyati -te	dṛṣṭvā	drakṣyati	see
√nī	nayati -te	nītvā	neṣyati	lead

√paṭh	paṭhati -te	paṭhitvā	paṭhiṣyati	read
√paś	paśyati -te	dṛṣṭvā	drakṣyati	see
√pā	pibati -te	pītvā	pāsyati	drink
√prach	pṛcchati -te	pṛṣṭvā	prakṣyati	ask
prati+√gam	pratigacchati	pratigatya pratigamya	pratigamiṣyati	return
√budh	bodhati -te	buddhvā	bodhiṣyati	know
√bhāṣ	bhāṣate -ti	bhāṣitvā	bhāṣiṣyate	speak
√bhū	bhavati -te	bhūtvā	bhaviṣyati	be
√man	manyate -ti	matvā	maṃsyate	think
√ram	ramate -ti	ratvā	raṃsyate	enjoy
√labh	labhate -ti	labdhvā	lapsyate	obtain
√vad	vadati -te	uditvā	vadiṣyati	speak
√vas	vasati -te	uṣitvā	vatsyati	live
√śubh	śobhate -ti	śobhitvā	śobhiṣyati	shine
√sev	sevate -ti	sevitvā	seviṣyate	serve

√sthā	tiṣṭhati -te	sthitvā	sthāsyati	stand
√smi	smayate -ti	smitvā	smeṣyate	smile
√smṛ	smarati -te	smṛtvā	smariṣyati	remember
√has	hasati -te	hasitvā	hasiṣyati	laugh

√as

PRESENT INDICATIVE

	Singular	Dual	Plural
Third	अस्ति asti	स्तः staḥ	सन्ति santi
Second	असि asi	स्थः sthaḥ	स्थ stha
First	अस्मि asmi	स्वः svaḥ	स्मः smaḥ

IMPERFECT

	Singular	Dual	Plural
3rd	आसीत् āsīt	आस्ताम् āstām	आसन् āsan
2nd	आसीः āsīḥ	आस्तम् āstam	आस्त āsta
1st	आसम् āsam	आस्व āsva	आस्म āsma

√gam

PRESENT ACTIVE

Stem: √**gam** (active) go

	Singular	Dual	Plural
3rd	गच्छति **gacchati**	गच्छतः **gacchataḥ**	गच्छन्ति **gacchanti**
2nd	गच्छसि **gacchasi**	गच्छथः **gacchathaḥ**	गच्छथ **gacchatha**
1st	गच्छामि **gacchāmi**	गच्छावः **gacchāvaḥ**	गच्छामः **gacchāmaḥ**

IMPERFECT ACTIVE

	Singular	Dual	Plural
3rd	अगच्छत् **agacchat**	अगच्छताम् **agacchatām**	अगच्छन् **agacchan**
2nd	अगच्छस् **agacchas**	अगच्छतम् **agacchatam**	अगच्छत **agacchata**
1st	अगच्छम् **agaccham**	अगच्छाव **agacchāva**	अगच्छाम **agacchāma**

√bhāṣ

Stem: bhāṣ (middle) speak

PRESENT MIDDLE

	Singular	Dual	Plural
3rd	भाषते bhāṣate	भाषेते bhāṣete	भाषन्ते bhāṣante
2nd	भाषसे bhāṣase	भाषेथे bhāṣethe	भाषध्वे bhāṣadhve
1st	भाषे bhāṣe	भाषावहे bhāṣāvahe	भाषामहे bhāṣāmahe

IMPERFECT MIDDLE

	Singular	Dual	Plural
3rd	अभाषत abhāṣata	अभाषेताम् abhāṣetām	अभाषन्त abhāṣanta
2nd	अभाषथाः abhāṣathāḥ	अभाषेथाम् abhāṣethām	अभाषध्वम् abhāṣadhvam
1st	अभाषे abhāṣe	अभाषावहि abhāṣāvahi	अभाषामहि abhāṣāmahi

PREFIXES

अति	ati	across, beyond, surpassing
अधि	adhi	above, over, on
अनु	anu	after, following
अन्तर्	antar	within, between
अप	apa	away, off
अपि	api	on, close on
अभि	abhi	to, against
अव	ava	down, away, off
आ	ā	back, return
उद्	ud	up, up out
उप	upa	towards
नि	ni	down, into
निस्	nis	out, forth
परा	parā	away, forth
परि	pari	around, about
प्र	pra	forward, onward, forth
प्रति	prati	back to, in reverse direction
वि	vi	apart, away, out
सम्	sam	together

NUMERALS

CARDINAL NUMBERS

	Numerals	Cardinal Numbers	
1.	१ (१)	one	**eka**
2.	२	two	**dvi**
3.	३	three	**tri**
4.	४	four	**catur**
5.	५ (५)	five	**pañca**
6.	६	six	**ṣaṣ**
7.	७	seven	**sapta**
8.	८ (८)	eight	**aṣṭa**
9.	९ (९)	nine	**nava**
10.	१०	ten	**daśa**

ORDINAL NUMBERS

First	**prathama**	Sixth	**ṣaṣṭha**
Second	**dvitīya**	Seventh	**saptama**
Third	**tṛtīya**	Eighth	**aṣṭama**
Fourth	**caturtha** (or **turīya**)	Ninth	**navama**
Fifth	**pañcama**	Tenth	**daśama**

SANDHI VOWELS

FINAL VOWELS: ā̆	ī̆	ū̆	ṛ	e	ai	au	INITIAL VOWELS
ā	ya	va	ra	e '	ā a	āva	**a**
ā	yā	vā	rā	a ā	ā ā	āvā	**ā**
e	ī	vī̆	rī̆	a ī̆	ā ī̆	āvī̆	**ī̆**
o	yū̆	ū	rū̆	a ū̆	ā ū̆	āvū̆	**ū̆**
ar	yṛ	vṛ	ṝ	a ṛ	ā ṛ	āvṛ	**ṛ**
ai	ye	ve	re	a e	ā e	āve	**e**
ai	yai	vai	rai	a ai	ā ai	āvai	**ai**
au	yo	vo	ro	a o	ā o	āvo	**o**
au	yau	vau	rau	a au	ā au	āvau	**au**

SANDHI FINAL S

Final letters of first word:

Any vowel **s** or **r** (except **as** and **ās**)	**ās**	**as**	Initial letter of second word:	
r	**ā**	**a**[2]	vowels	(a)
r	**ā**	**o**	**g/gh**	
r	**ā**	**o**	**j/jh**	
r	**ā**	**o**	**ḍ/ḍh**	
r	**ā**	**o**	**d/dh**	
r	**ā**	**o**	**b/bh**	(b)
r	**ā**	**o**	**nasals** (n/m)	
r	**ā**	**o**	**y/v**	
zero[1]	**ā**	**o**	**r**	
r	**ā**	**o**	**l**	
r	**ā**	**o**	**h**	
ḥ	**āḥ**	**aḥ**	**k/kh**	
ś	**āś**	**aś**	**c/ch**	
ṣ	**āṣ**	**aṣ**	**ṭ/ṭh**	
s	**ās**	**as**	**t/th**	
ḥ	**āḥ**	**aḥ**	**p/ph**	(c)
ḥ	**āḥ**	**aḥ**	**ś**	
ḥ	**āḥ**	**aḥ**	**ṣ/s**	
ḥ	**āḥ**	**aḥ**	**end of line**	

(1) The **s** disappears, and if **i** or **u** precedes, it becomes **ī** or **ū**.

The **r** disappears, and if **a**, **i**, or **u** precedes, it becomes **ā**, **ī**, or **ū**.

(2) Except that **as** + **a** = **o '** For example:

रामस् + अत्र = रामो ऽत्र

rāmas + atra = rāmo 'tra

Remember that **ḥ** follows the same rules as final **s**.

SANDHI
FINAL S

					a	**ā**		
					i	**ī**		
					u	**ū**	(a)	
					ṛ	**ṝ**	Vowels	
					ḷ			
					e	**ai**		
					o	**au**		
ḥ		**ka**	**kha**	|	**ga**	**gha**	**ṅa**	
ś		**ca**	**cha**	|	**ja**	**jha**	**ña**	
ṣ		**ṭa**	**ṭha**	|	**ḍa**	**ḍha**	**ṇa**	
s		**ta**	**tha**	|	**da**	**dha**	**na**	
ḥ		**pa**	**pha**	|	**ba**	**bha**	**ma**	
				|	**ya**	**ra**	**la**	**va**
ḥ	**śa**	**ṣa**	**sa**	|	**ha**			
ḥ	end of line			|				
	(c) Unvoiced consonant			|	(b) Voiced consonant			

(a) If the second word begins in a vowel:
  as becomes **a** (except **as** + **a** = **o** ')
  ās becomes **ā**
  vowel **s** becomes **r**

(b) If the first letter of the second word is a voiced consonant:
  as becomes **o**
  ās becomes **ā**
  vowel **s** becomes **r** (except before a word beginning in **r**)

(c) If the first letter of the second word is an unvoiced consonant, the **s** (with any vowel is in front of it) changes to the letter in the far left column.

SANDHI FINAL M, N, T

FINAL LETTER OF FIRST WORD: t	n	m	INITIAL LETTER OF SECOND WORD:
d	n[1]	m	vowels
d	n	ṃ	g/gh
j	ñ	ṃ	j/jh
ḍ	ṇ	ṃ	ḍ/ḍh
d	n	ṃ	d/dh
d	n	ṃ	b/bh
n	n	ṃ	nasals (n/m)
d	n	ṃ	y/v
d	n	ṃ	r
l	ṃl	ṃ	l
d(dh)[3]	n	ṃ	h
t	n	ṃ	k/kh
c	ṃś	ṃ	c/ch
ṭ	ṃṣ	ṃ	ṭ/ṭh
t	ṃs	ṃ	t/th
t	n	ṃ	p/ph
c(ch)[4]	ñ (ch)[2]	ṃ	ś
t	n	ṃ	ṣ/s
t	n	m	end of line

1. If the vowel before the **n** is short, the **n** becomes **nn**.
2. The following **ś** may become **ch**.
3. The following **h** becomes **dh**.
4. The following **ś** becomes **ch**

SANDHI
FINAL N

Final **n** remains unchanged unless the following letter is in bold. Then,

n becomes								**n** becomes
			|	**a**	**ā**			
			|	**i**	**ī**			
			|	**u**	**ū**			**nn** (e)
			|	**ṛ**	**ṝ**			(if preceded by
			|	**ḷ**				a short vowel)
			|	**e**	**ai**			
			|	**o**	**au**			
	ka	kha	|	ga	gha	na		
(a) **ṃś**	**ca**	**cha**	|	**ja**	**jha**	ña		**ñ** (f)
(b) **ṃṣ**	**ṭa**	**ṭha**	|	**ḍa**	**ḍha**	ṇa		**ṇ** (g)
(c) **ṃs**	**ta**	**tha**	|	da	dha	na		
	pa	pha	|	ba	bha	ma		
			|	ya	ra	**la**	va	**ṃl** (h)
(d) **ñ** (ch) **śa**	ṣa	sa	|	ha				
	end of line							

(a) **n + ca = ṃśca ; n + cha = ṃścha**

(b) **n + ṭa = ṃṣṭa ; n + ṭha = ṃṣṭha**

(c) **n + ta = ṃsta ; n + tha = ṃstha**

(d) **n + śa = ñśa** or **ñcha**

(e) **an + a = anna**

an + i = anni

ān + u = ānu

(f) **n + ja = ñja ; n + jha = ñjha**

(g) **n + ḍa = ṇḍa ; n + ḍha = ṇḍha**

(h) **n + la = ṃlla**

SANDHI FINAL T

t remains t except:							t changes to d except:
			a	ā			
			i	ī			
			u	ū			
			ṛ	ṝ			
			ḷ				
			e	ai			
			o	au			(before all nasals)
							n (d)
	ka	kha	ga	gha	**na**		
(a) **c**	**ca**	**cha**	**ja**	**jha**	**ña**		**j** (e)
(b) **ṭ**	**ṭa**	**ṭha**	**ḍa**	**ḍha**	**ṇa**		**ḍ** (f)
	ta	tha	da	dha	**na**		
	pa	pha	ba	bha	**ma**		
			ya	ra	**la**	va	**l** (g)
(c) **c** (**ch**) **śa**	ṣa	sa	**ha**				**d** (**dh**) (h)
	end of line						

(a) **t + ca = cca ; t + cha = ccha**

(b) **t + ṭa = ṭṭa ; t + ṭha = ṭṭha**

(c) **ṭ + śa = ccha**

(d) **t +** all nasals **= nnasal**

(e) **t + ja = jja ; t + jha = jjha**

(f) **t + ḍa = ḍḍa ; t + ḍha = ḍḍha**

(g) **t + la = lla**

(h) **t + ha = ddha** (The **h** becomes **dh**.)

SANDHI FINAL M

(a) If the next word begins in a consonant, the **m** becomes **ṃ** and is pronounced (and could be written) as the nasal corresponding to the first letter of the next word.

(b) If the next word begins in a vowel or is at the end of a line, the **m** remains the same. The **m** remains the same because the mouth is not preparing to close at a specific point of contact as it would if the next word began with a consonant.

SANDHI FINAL R

(a) Before a word beginning with a voiced letter (other than **r**), the **r** remains the same.

(b) Before an unvoiced letter or the end of a line, **r** follows the same rules as final **s**.

(c) Final **r**, whether original or derived from **s**, cannot stand before another **r**. The final **r** is dropped and the vowel before it made long if it is short.

FINAL P, Ṭ, K

(a) Before a voiced sound these letters become voiced, and before an unvoiced sound they remain the same.

(b) Before a nasal these letters become the nasal of their row (**varga**).

(c) Before **h** these letters become voiced and the **h** becomes their voiced aspirated counterpart.

FINAL Ṅ

(a) Like final **n**, final **ṅ** becomes **ṅṅ** before vowels if the **ṅ** is preceded by a short vowel.

INITIAL CH

(a) Initial **ch** becomes **cch** if the first word ends in a short vowel. The **ch** also becomes **cch** after the preposition **ā** and **mā**.

INTERNAL SANDHI

S TO Ṣ

any vowel (but **a** or **ā**), **k**, or **r**	in spite of intervening **ṃ** or **ḥ**	changes **s** to **ṣ**	unless final or followed by **r**

N TO Ṇ

r **ṛ** or **ṣ**	unless **c**, **ch**, **j**, **jh**, **ñ**, **ṭ**, **ṭh**, **ḍ**, **ḍh**, **ṇ**, **t**, **th**, **d**, **dh**, **l**, **ś**, **s** interferes	changes **n** to **ṇ**	if followed by vowels, **m**, **y**, **v**, or **n**

VOCABULARY

अग्नि	**agni** (mas)	fire
अति	**ati** (prefix)	across, beyond, surpassing
अतिथि	**atithi** (mas)	guest
अतीव	**atīva** (ind)	very
अत्र	**atra** (ind)	here
अधि	**adhi** (prefix)	above, over, on
अनु	**anu** (prefix)	after, following
अन्तर्	**antar** (prefix)	within, between
अप	**apa** (prefix)	away, off
अपि	**api** (prefix)	on, close on
अपि	**api** (ind)	also, too
अभि	**abhi** (prefix)	to, against
अमृतम्	**amṛtam** (neuter)	immortality
अल्प	**alpa** mf(**ā**)n (adj)	little
अव	**ava** (prefix)	down, away, off
अव गम्	**ava** + √**gam avagacchati**	he understands
अविद्या	**avidyā** (fem)	ignorance

अश्व	**aśva** (mas)	horse
अष्ट	**aṣṭa**	eight
अष्टम	**aṣṭama** mf(ī)n (adj)	eighth
अस्	**√as asti**	he, she, it is
असिद्धि	**asiddhi** (mas)	failure
अस्मद्	**asmad** (pro)	we (used in compounds)
अहो	**aho** (ind)	aha, hey!
आ	**ā** (prefix)	back, return
आ गम्	**ā + √gam āgacchati**	he comes
आ नी	**ā + √nī ānayati**	he brings
आचार्य	**ācārya** (mas)	teacher
आत्मन्	**ātman** (mas)	Self
इति	**iti** (ind)	(end of quote)
इव	**iva** (ind)	as if, like
उद्	**ud** (prefix)	up, up out
उद् भू	**ud + √bhū udbhavati**	he is born
उद् स्था	**ud + √sthā uttiṣṭhati**	he stands up

उप	**upa** (prefix)	towards
उप गम्	**upa** + √**gam** **upagacchati**	he goes toward, approaches
ऋषि	**ṛṣi** (mas)	seer, sage
एक	**eka**	one
एव	**eva** (ind)	only, ever
एवम्	**evam** (ind)	thus, in this way
कथम्	**katham** (ind)	how
कथा	**kathā** (fem)	story
कदा	**kadā** (ind)	when
कन्या	**kanyā** (fem)	girl
कर्तृ	**kartṛ** (mas)	maker, doer
कर्मन्	**karman** (neuter)	action
कवि	**kavi** (mas)	poet
कुत्र	**kutra** (ind)	where
कुपित	**kupita** mf(**ā**)n (adj)	angry
कुलम्	**kulam** (neuter)	family
कीर्ति	**kīrti** (fem)	glory, fame

कृष्ण	**kṛṣṇa** (mas noun) mf(**ā**)n adj	Kṛṣṇa, black
गज	**gaja** (mas)	elephant
गम्	√**gam** **gacchati -te**	he goes
गुप्	√**gup** **gopayati -te**	he protects
गुरु	**guru** (mas noun) mf(**vī**)n adj	teacher, heavy
गृहम्	**gṛham** (neuter)	house
ग्राम	**grāma** (mas)	village
च	**ca** (ind)	and
चतुर्	**catur**	four
चतुर्थ	**caturtha** mf(ī)n (adj)	fourth
चन्द्र	**candra** (mas)	moon
चिन्त्	√**cint** **cintayati -te**	he thinks
छाया	**chāyā** (fem)	shadow
जलम्	**jalam** (neuter)	water
जि	√**ji** **jayati -te**	he conquers
ज्ञानम्	**jñānam** (neuter)	knowledge
ततः	**tataḥ** (ind)	therefore

तत्र	**tatra** (ind)	there
तथा	**tathā** (ind)	so, therefore
तद्	**tad** (pro)	he, she, it (used in compounds)
तदा	**tadā** (ind)	then
तुरीय	**turīya** mf(ā)n (adj)	fourth
तृतीय	**tṛtīya** mf(ā)n (adj)	third
त्वद्	**tvad** (pro)	you (used in compounds)
त्रि	**tri**	three
दश	**daśa**	ten
दशम	**daśama** mf(ī)n (adj)	tenth
दातृ	**dātṛ** (mas)	giver
दात्री	**dātrī** (fem)	giver
दुःखम्	**duḥkham** (neuter)	suffering
दृश्	**√dṛś paśyati -te**	he sees
द्वि	**dvi**	two
द्वितीय	**dvitīya** mf(ā)n (adj)	second

धार्मिक	**dhārmika** mf(ī)n (adj)	virtuous
धेनु	**dhenu** (fem)	cow
न	**na** (ind)	not
नदी	**nadī** (fem)	river
नर	**nara** (mas)	man
नव	**nava**	nine
नवम	**navama** mf(ī)n (adj)	ninth
नाम	**nāma** (ind)	by name
नामन्	**nāman** (neuter)	name
नि	**ni** (prefix)	down, into
निस्	**nis** (prefix)	out, forth
नी	**√nī nayati -te**	he leads
नृप	**nṛpa** (mas)	king
पञ्च	**pañca**	five
पञ्चम	**pañcama** mf(ī)n (adj)	fifth
पठ्	**√paṭh paṭhati -te**	he reads
पत्नी	**patnī** (fem)	wife

परा	**parā** (prefix)	away, forth
परि	**pari** (prefix)	around, about
पश्	**√paś paśyati -te**	he sees
पा	**√pā pibati -te**	he drinks
पितृ	**pitṛ** (mas)	father
पुत्र	**putra** (mas)	son
पुत्रिका	**putrikā** (fem)	daughter
पुनर्	**punar** (ind)	again
पुस्तकम्	**pustakam** (neuter)	book
पूर्ण	**pūrṇa** mf(**ā**)n (adj or noun)	full, fullness
प्र	**pra** (prefix)	forward, onward, forth
प्रछ्	**√prach pṛcchati -te**	he asks
प्रजा	**prajā** (fem)	child, subject (of a king)
प्रति	**prati** (prefix)	back to, in reverse direction
प्रति गम्	**prati** + **√gam pratigacchati**	he goes back, returns

प्रथम	**prathama** mf(**ā**)n (adj)	first
प्रिय	**priya** mf(**ā**)n (adj)	dear, beloved
फलम्	**phalam** (neuter)	fruit
बहु	**bahu** mf(**vī** or **u**) n (adj)	much, many
बाल	**bāla** (mas)	boy
बाला	**bālā** (fem)	girl
बुध्	**√budh bodhati -te**	he knows
भार्या	**bhāryā** (fem)	wife
भाष्	**√bhāṣ bhāṣate -ti**	he speaks
भीत	**bhīta** mf(**ā**)n (adj)	afraid
भू	**√bhū bhavati -te**	he is
भूमि	**bhūmi** (fem)	earth
भ्रातृ	**bhrātṛ** (mas)	brother
मद्	**mad** (pro)	I (used in compounds)
मन्	**√man manyate -ti**	he thinks
मातृ	**mātṛ** (fem)	mother
माला	**mālā** (fem)	garland

मित्रम्	**mitram** (neuter)	friend
मृग	**mṛga** (mas)	deer
यतः	**yataḥ** (ind)	since
यत्र	**yatra** (ind)	where
यथा	**yathā** (ind)	since, as
यद्	**yad** (rel pro)	who, what, which (declined like **tad**)
यदा	**yadā** (ind)	when
यदि	**yadi** (ind)	if
युष्मद्	**yuṣmad** (pro)	you (used in compounds)
रम्	**√ram ramate -ti**	he enjoys
रमणीय	**ramaṇīya** mf(**ā**)n (adj)	pleasant
राजन्	**rājan** (mas)	king
राम	**rāma** (mas)	Rāma
लभ्	**√labh labhate -ti**	he obtains
वद्	**√vad vadati -te**	he speaks
वनम्	**vanam** (neuter)	forest

वस्	**√vas vasati -te**	he lives
वा	**vā** (ind)	or
वापी	**vāpī** (fem)	pond
वि	**vi** (prefix)	apart, away, out
विद्या	**vidyā** (fem)	knowledge
विना	**vinā** (ind)	without
वीर	**vīra** (mas)	hero
शत्रु	**śatru** (mas)	enemy
शान्ति	**śānti** (fem)	peace
शास्त्रम्	**śāstram** (neuter)	scripture
शिष्य	**śiṣya** (mas)	student
शीघ्र	**śīghra** mf(**ā**)n (adj)	swift
शुक्ल	**śukla** mf(**ā**)n (adj)	white
शुभ्	**√śubh śobhate -ti**	he shines
शोभन	**śobhana** mf(**ā** or **ī**)n (adj)	shining, bright, beautiful
षष्	**ṣaṣ**	six
षष्ठ	**ṣaṣṭha** mf(**ī**)n(adj)	sixth

सत्यम्	**satyam** (neuter)	truth
सप्त	**sapta**	seven
सप्तम	**saptama** mf(ī)n (adj)	seventh
सम्	**sam** (prefix)	together
सह	**saha** (ind)	with
सिद्ध	**siddha** mf(ā)	one who attains perfection
सिद्धि	**siddhi** (mas)	perfection, attainment, proof
सीता	**sītā** (fem)	Sītā
सुखम्	**sukham** (neuter)	happiness
सुन्दर	**sundara** mf(ī)n (adj)	beautiful
सूक्तम्	**sūktam** (neuter)	hymn
सूर्य	**sūrya** (mas)	sun
सेना	**senā** (fem)	army
सेव्	**√sev sevate -ti**	he serves
स्था	**√sthā tiṣṭhati -te**	he stands
स्मि	**√smi smayate -ti**	he smiles

स्मृ	√**smṛ smarati -te**	he remembers
स्वसृ	**svasṛ** (fem)	sister
हस्	√**has hasati -te**	he laughs
हस्त	**hasta** (mas)	hand
हेतु	**hetu** (mas)	cause, motive

ENGLISH-SANSKRIT VOCABULARY

above, over, on	अधि	**adhi** (prefix)
across, beyond, surpassing	अति	**ati** (prefix)
action	कर्मन्	**karman** (neuter)
afraid	भीत	**bhīta** mf(**ā**)n (adj)
after, following	अनु	**anu** (prefix)
again	पुनर्	**punar** (ind)
aha, hey!	अहो	**aho** (ind)
also, too	अपि	**api** (ind)
and	च	**ca** (ind)
angry	कुपित	**kupita** mf(**ā**)n (adj)
apart, away, out	वि	**vi** (prefix)
army	सेना	**senā** (fem)
around, about	परि	**pari** (prefix)
as if, like	इव	**iva** (ind)
ask	प्रछ्	**√prach pṛcchati -te**
away, forth	परा	**parā** (prefix)
away, off	अप	**apa** (prefix)

back, return	आ	**ā** (prefix)
back to, in reverse direction	प्रति	**prati** (prefix)
beautiful	सुन्दर	**sundara** mf(**ī**)n (adj)
book	पुस्तकम्	**pustakam** (neuter)
born	उद् भू	**ud** + √**bhū** **udbhavati**
boy	बाल	**bāla** (mas)
bring	आ नी	**ā** + √**nī** **ānayati**
brother	भ्रातृ	**bhrātṛ** (mas)
by name, named	नाम	**nāma** (ind)
cause, motive	हेतु	**hetu** (mas)
child, subject (of a king)	प्रजा	**prajā** (fem)
come	आ गम्	**ā** + √**gam** **āgacchati**
conquer	जि	√**ji** **jayati -te**
cow	धेनु	**dhenu** (fem)
daughter	पुत्रिका	**putrikā** (fem)
dear, beloved	प्रिय	**priya** mf(**ā**)n (adj)

deer	मृग	**mṛga** (mas)
down	अव	**ava** (prefix)
down, into	नि	**ni** (prefix)
drink	पा	√pā pibati -te
earth	भूमि	**bhūmi** (fem)
eight	अष्ट	**aṣṭa**
eighth	अष्टम	**aṣṭama** mf(ī)n (adj)
elephant	गज	**gaja** (mas)
(end of quote)	इति	**iti** (ind)
enemy	शत्रु	**śatru** (mas)
enjoy	रम्	√ram ramate -ti
failure	असिद्धि	**asiddhi** (mas)
family	कुलम्	**kulam** (neuter)
father	पितृ	**pitṛ** (mas)
fifth	पञ्चम	**pañcama** mf(ī)n (adj)
fire	अग्नि	**agni** (mas)

first	प्रथम	**prathama** mf(ā)n (adj)
five	पञ्च	**pañca**
forest	वनम्	**vanam** (neuter)
forward, onward, forth	प्र	**pra** (prefix)
four	चतुर्	**catur**
fourth	चतुर्थ	**caturtha** mf(ī)n (adj)
fourth	तुरीय	**turīya** mf(ā)n (adj)
friend	मित्रम्	**mitram** (neuter)
fruit	फलम्	**phalam** (neuter)
full, fullness	पूर्ण	**pūrṇa** mf(ā)n (adj)
garland	माला	**mālā** (fem)
girl	कन्या	**kanyā** (fem)
girl	बाला	**bālā** (fem)
giver	दातृ	**dātṛ** (mas)
giver	दात्री	**dātrī** (fem)
glory, fame	कीर्ति	**kīrti** (fem)

go	गम्	**√gam gacchati -te**
go back, return	प्रति गम्	**prati + √gam pratigacchati**
go toward, approach	उप गम्	**upa + √gam upagacchati**
guest	अतिथि	**atithi** (mas)
hand	हस्त	**hasta** (mas)
happiness	सुखम्	**sukham** (neuter)
he (see declension)	तद्	**tad** (pro)
here	अत्र	**atra** (ind)
hero	वीर	**vīra** (mas)
horse	अश्व	**aśva** (mas)
house	गृहम्	**gṛham** (neuter)
how	कथम्	**katham** (ind)
hymn	सूक्तम्	**sūktam** (neuter)
I (used in compounds)	मद्	**mad** (pro)
if	यदि	**yadi** (ind)
ignorance	अविद्या	**avidyā** (fem)

immortality	अमृतम्	**amṛtam** (neuter)
is	अस्	√as asti
is	भू	√bhū bhavati -te
it (used in compounds)	तद्	**tad** (pro)
king	नृप	**nṛpa** (mas)
king	राजन्	**rājan** (mas)
know	बुध्	√budh bodhati -te
knowledge	ज्ञानम्	**jñānam** (neuter)
knowledge	विद्या	**vidyā** (fem)
Kṛṣṇa, black	कृष्ण	**kṛṣṇa** (mas noun) or mf(**ā**)n (adj)
laugh	हस्	√has hasati -te
lead	नी	√nī nayati -te
little	अल्प	**alpa** mf(**ā**)n (adj)
live	वस्	√vas vasati -te
maker, doer	कर्तृ	**kartṛ** (mas)
man	नर	**nara** (mas)

moon	चन्द्र	**candra** (mas)
mother	मातृ	**mātṛ** (fem)
much, many	बहु	**bahu** mf(**vī** or **u**) n (adj)
name	नामन्	**nāman** (neuter)
nine	नव	**nava**
ninth	नवम	**navama** mf(ī)n
not	न	**na** (ind)
obtain	लभ्	**√labh labhate -ti**
on, close on	अपि	**api** (prefix)
one	एक	**eka**
one who attains perfection	सिद्ध	**siddha** mf(**ā**)
only, ever (emphatic)	एव	**eva** (ind)
or	वा	**vā** (ind)
out, forth	निस्	**nis** (prefix)
peace	शान्ति	**śānti** (fem)
perfection, attainment, proof	सिद्धि	**siddhi** (mas)

pleasant	रमणीय	**ramaṇīya** mf(ā)n (adj)
poet	कवि	**kavi** (mas)
pond	वापी	**vāpī** (fem)
protect	गुप्	**√gup gopayati -te**
Rāma	राम	**rāma** (mas)
read	पठ्	**√paṭh paṭhati -te**
remember	स्मृ	**√smṛ smarati -te**
river	नदी	**nadī** (fem)
scripture, text	शास्त्रम्	**śāstram** (neuter)
second	द्वितीय	**dvitīya** mf(ā)n (adj)
see	दृश्	**√dṛś paśyati -te** or
	पश्	**√paś paśyati -te**
seer, sage	ऋषि	**ṛṣi** (mas)
Self	आत्मन्	**ātman** (mas)
serve	सेव्	**√sev sevate -ti**
seven	सप्त	**sapta**
seventh	सप्तम	**saptama** mf(ī)n (adj)

shadow	छाया	**chāyā** (fem)
she (see declension)	तद्	**tad** (pro)
shine	शुभ्	**√śubh śobhate -ti**
shining, bright, beautiful	शोभन	**śobhana** mf(ā or ī)n (adj)
since	यतः	**yataḥ** (ind)
since, as	यथा	**yathā** (ind)
sister	स्वसृ	**svasṛ** (fem)
Sītā	सीता	**sītā** (fem)
six	षष्	**ṣaṣ**
sixth	षष्ठ	**ṣaṣṭha** mf(ī)n(adj)
smile	स्मि	**√smi smayate -ti**
so, therefore	तथा	**tathā** (ind)
son	पुत्र	**putra** (mas)
speak	भाष्	**√bhāṣ bhāṣate -ti**
speak	वद्	**√vad vadati -te**
stand	स्था	**√sthā tiṣṭhati -te**

stand up	उद् स्था	**ud** + √**sthā** **uttiṣṭhati**
story	कथा	**kathā** (fem)
student	शिष्य	**śiṣya** (mas)
suffering	दुःखम्	**duḥkham** (neuter)
sun	सूर्य	**sūrya** (mas)
swift	शीघ्र	**śīghra** mf(**ā**)n (adj)
teacher	आचार्य	**ācārya** (mas)
teacher, heavy	गुरु	**guru** (mas noun) or mf(**vī**)n (adj)
ten	दश	**daśa**
tenth	दशम	**daśama** mf(**ī**)n (adj)
then	तदा	**tadā** (ind)
there	तत्र	**tatra** (ind)
therefore	ततः	**tataḥ** (ind)
think	चिन्त्	√**cint** **cintayati** **-te**
think	मन्	√**man** **manyate** **-ti**
third	तृतीय	**tṛtīya** mf(**ā**)n (adj)

three	त्रि	**tri**
thus, in this way	एवम्	**evam** (ind)
to, against	अभि	**abhi** (prefix)
together	सम्	**sam** (prefix)
towards	उप	**upa** (prefix)
truth	सत्यम्	**satyam** (neuter)
two	द्वि	**dvi**
understand	अव गम्	**ava** + √**gam** **avagacchati**
up, up out	उद्	**ud** (prefix)
very	अतीव	**atīva** (ind)
village	ग्राम	**grāma** (mas)
virtuous	धार्मिक	**dhārmika** mf(ī)n (adj)
water	जलम्	**jalam** (neuter)
we (used in compounds)	अस्मद्	**asmad** (pro)
when (question)	कदा	**kadā** (ind)
when	यदा	**yadā** (ind)

where (question)	कुत्र	**kutra** (ind)
where	यत्र	**yatra** (ind)
white	शुक्ल	**śukla** mf(**ā**)n (adj)
who, what (declined like **tad**)	यद्	**yad** (rel pro)
with	सह	**saha** (ind)
within, between	अन्तर्	**antar** (prefix)
without	विना	**vinā** (ind)
wife	पत्नी	**patnī** (fem)
wife	भार्या	**bhāryā** (fem)
you (sing, used in compounds)	त्वद्	**tvad** (pro)
you (plural, used in compounds)	युष्मद्	**yuṣmad** (pro)

ऋचो अक्षरे परमे व्योमन्
यस्मिन्देवा अधि विश्वे निषेदुः ।
यस्तन्न वेद किमृचा करिष्यति
य इत्तद्विदुस्त इमे समासते ॥

ṛco akṣare parame vyoman
yasmin devā adhi viśve niṣeduḥ
yas tan na veda kim ṛcā kariṣyati
ya it tad vidus ta ime samāsate
Ṛg-Ved, 1.164.39

The verses of the Ved exist in the collapse of fullness in the transcendental field.
In which reside all the impulses of creative intelligence, the laws of nature, responsible for the whole manifest universe.
He whose awareness is not open to this field, what can the verses accomplish for him?
Those who know this level of reality are established in evenness, in wholeness of life.

ṛco	**akṣare**	**parame**	**vyoman**
verses	in the collapse of fullness	in the transcendental	field

yasmin	**devā**	**adhi**	**viśve**	**niṣeduḥ**
in which	impulses (laws of nature)	responsible for	universe	reside

yas	**tan**	**na veda**	**kim**	**ṛcā**	**kariṣyati**
who	this (field)	not know	what	verses	will accomplish

ya	**it**	**tad**	**vidus**	**ta**	**ime samāsate**
who	alone	this level	know	they	in evenness established

1. निस्त्रैगुण्यो भवार्जुन ।

nistraiguṇyo bhavārjuna

without three **guṇas** be O Arjuna

Be without the three guṇas, O Arjuna.

Bhagavad-Gītā, 2.45

2. योगस्थः कुरु कर्माणि ।

yogasthaḥ kuru karmāṇi

yoga established perform action

Established in being perform action.

Bhagavad-Gītā, 2.48

3. प्रकृतिं स्वामवष्टभ्य विसृजामि पुनः पुनः ।

prakṛtiṃ svām avaṣṭabhya visṛjāmi punaḥ punaḥ

nature own curving back I create again again

Curving back upon my own nature, I create again and again.

Bhagavad-Gītā, 9.8

4. मयाध्यक्षेण प्रकृतिः सूयते सचराचरम् ।

mayādhyakṣeṇa prakṛtiḥ sūyate sacarācaram

by my presidentship nature creates moving unmoving

Under my presidentship my nature (intelligence) creates the moving and the unmoving.

Bhagavad-Gītā, 9.10

Mahāvākyas Great Sayings

1. **अहं ब्रह्मास्मि ।**

ahaṃ brahmāsmi
I totality (wholeness) am
I am the totality.

Bṛhadāraṇyaka Upaniṣad, 1.4.10

2. **तत्त्वमसि ।**

tat tvam asi
that thou art
Thou art that.

Chāndogya Upaniṣad, 6.11

3. **सर्वं खल्विदं ब्रह्म ।**

sarvaṃ khalv idaṃ brahma (**hma** in this word is pronounced **mha**)
all (emphatic) this (is) brahman
All this is brahman.

Chāndogya Upaniṣad, 3.14.1

4. **प्रज्ञानं ब्रह्म ।**

prajñānaṃ brahma
consciousness (is) brahman
Consciousness is brahman.

Aitareya Upaniṣad, 3.1.3

1. पूर्णमदः पूर्णमिदं पूर्णात्पूर्णमुदच्यते ।
पूर्णस्य पूर्णमादाय पूर्णमेवावशिष्यते ॥

pūrṇam adaḥ pūrṇam idaṃ pūrṇāt pūrṇam udacyate
pūrṇasya pūrṇam ādāya pūrṇam evāvaśiṣyate

Īśa Upaniṣad, (introductory verse for several ***Upaniṣads***)

pūrṇam adaḥ pūrṇam idaṃ pūrṇāt pūrṇam udacyate
full (is) that full (is) this from fullness fullness comes out

pūrṇasya pūrṇam ādāya pūrṇam evāvaśiṣyate
of fullness fullness taking fullness remains

That is full; this is full. From fullness, fullness comes out.
Taking fullness from fullness, what remains is fullness.

2. वसुधैव कुटुम्बकम् ।
vasudhaiva kuṭumbakam
the world family
The world is my family.

Manu Śmṛti, 11.12.22

1. योगश्चित्तवृत्तिनिरोधः ।

yogaś citta-vṛtti-nirodhaḥ

yoga mind-fluctuation-least excited

Yoga is the least excited state of the mind.

***Yoga Sūtras*, 1.2**

2. हेयं दुःखमनागतम् ।

heyaṃ duḥkham anāgatam

avert (to be averted) danger not yet come

Avert the danger which has not yet come.

***Yoga Sūtras*, 2.16**

3. तत्सृष्ट्वा तदेवानुप्राविशत् ।

tat sṛṣṭvā tad evānuprāviśat

it having created it entered into

Having created it, the Creator entered into it.

***Taitirīya Upaniṣad*, 2.6.1**

4. भगवद्गीता किञ्चिदधीता ।

गङ्गाजललवकणिका पीता ॥

bhagavad-gītā kiñcid adhītā

gaṅgā-jala-lava-kaṇikā pītā

Bhagavad-Gītā a little studied

Ganges-water-drop-particle drank.

Even a little study of the ***Bhagavad-Gītā,***

like a drop of the flow of nectar, is sufficient for enlightenment.

Śaṅkara, ***Bhaja Govindam***, 20

सह नाववतु ।

सह नौ भुनक्तु ।

सह वीर्यं करवावहै ।

तेजस्वि नावधीतमस्तु ।

मा विद्विषावहै ॥

saha nāv avatu

saha nau bhunaktu

saha vīryaṃ karavāvahai

tejasvi nāv adhītam astu

mā vidviṣāvahai

Upaniṣads (introduction for several ***Upaniṣads***)

Let us be together,

Let us eat together,

Let us be vital together,

Let us be radiating truth,
radiating the light of life,

Never shall we denounce anyone,
never entertain negativity.

1. सत्यं ब्रूयात्प्रियं ब्रूयात् ।

satyaṃ brūyāt priyaṃ brūyāt

truth speak sweetness speak

Speak the sweet truth.

Manu Smṛti, 2.161

2. ब्रह्मवित् ब्रह्मैव भवति ।

brahmavit brahmaiva bhavati

brahman knower brahman becomes

The knower of brahman becomes brahman.

Muṇḍaka Upaniṣad, 3.2.9

3. द्वितीयाद्वै भयं भवति ।

dvitīyād vai bhayaṃ bhavati

from duality certainly fear is

Certainly fear is born of duality.

Bṛhadāraṇyaka Upaniṣad, 1.4.2

4. यो जागार तमृचः कामयन्ते ।

yo jāgāra tam ṛcaḥ kāmayante

who is awake him hymns seek out

He who is awake, the ṛcas seek him out.

Ṛg-Ved, 5.44.14

5. निवर्तध्वम् ।

nivartadhvam

Transcend. *Ṛg-Ved*, 10.19.1

यस्य निश्वसितं वेदाः
यो वेदेभ्यो ऽखिलं जगत् ।
निर्ममे तमहं वन्दे
विद्यातीर्थमहेश्वरम् ॥

yasya niśvasitaṃ vedāḥ
yo vedebhyo 'khilaṃ jagat
nirmame tam ahaṃ vande
vidyā-tīrtha-maheśvaram

Sāyaṇa, ***Ṛg-Ved Bhāṣya***, Introduction

I bow down to him who breathes out the Ved
and creates the universe from it,
remaining uninvolved, and who is the cherished shrine
of pilgrimage for all the streams of knowledge.

yasya	**niśvasitaṃ**	**vedāḥ**
whose	breath (is)	the Ved

yo vedebhyo	**'khilaṃ**	**jagat**
who from the Ved	entire	universe

nirmame	**tam**	**ahaṃ**	**vande**
creates (remaining uninvolved)	to him	I	bow down

vidyā	**tīrtha**	**maheśvaram**
knowledge	shrine of pilgrimage	

1. एकमेवाद्वितीयम् ।

ekam evādvitīyam

one no second

One without a second.

Chāndogya Upaniṣad, 6.2.1

2. अणोरणीयान्महतोमहीयान् ।

aṇoraṇīyān mahatomahīyān

than small smaller than large larger

Smaller than the smallest, larger than the largest.

Kaṭha Upaniṣad, 1.2.20

3. तत्सन्निधौ वैरत्यागः ।

tat-sannidhau vaira-tyāgaḥ

that-vicinity diversifying tendencies-lost

In the vicinity of coherence, hostile tendencies are eliminated.

Yoga Sūtras, 2.35

4. आत्मा वारे द्रष्टव्यः श्रोतव्यो मन्तव्यो
निदिध्यासितव्यः

ātmā vāre draṣṭavyaḥ śrotavyo mantavyo
nididhyāsitavyaḥ

That atman alone, that state of simplest form of awareness alone, is worthy of seeing, hearing, contemplating, and realizing.

Bṛhadāraṇyaka Upaniṣad, 2.4.5

5. सत्यमेव जयते

satyam eva jayate

Truth alone triumphs. *Muṇḍaka Upaniṣad*, 3.1.6

1. असतो मा सद्गमय ।

तमसो मा ज्योतिर्गमय ।

मृत्योर्मामृतं गमय ॥

asato mā sad gamaya
tamaso mā jyotir gamaya
mṛtyor mā amṛtaṃ gamaya

Bṛhadāraṇyaka Upaniṣad, 1.3.28

From non-existence lead us to existence,
From darkness lead us to light,
From death lead us to immortality.

asato	**mā**	**sad**	**gamaya**
from non-existence	me	existence	lead
tamaso	**mā**	**jyotir**	**gamaya**
from darkness	me	light	lead
mṛtyor	**mā**	**amṛtaṃ**	**gamaya**
from death	me	immortality	lead

2. आयुर्वेदो ऽमृतानाम् ।

āyur-vedo 'mṛtānām
(āyur-ved amṛtānām)
Āyur-Ved is for those who desire immortality.

***Caraka Saṃhitā*, Sūtrasthāna**, 25.40

1 तिलेषु तैलवद्वेदे वेदान्तः सुप्रतिष्ठितः ।

tileṣu tailavad vede vedāntaḥ supratiṣṭhitaḥ

in a sesame seed oil like in Ved Vedanta is established

As oil is present in a sesame seed, so is wholeness present in the Ved.

Mukitkā Upaniṣad, 1.9

2. एकं सद्विप्रा बहुधा वदन्ति ।

ekaṃ sad viprā bahudhā vadanti

one truth different names wise call

Truth is one; the wise call it by different names.

Ṛg-Ved, 1.164.46

3. भूमिरापो ऽनलो वायुः

खं मनो बुद्धिरेव च ।

अहंकार इतीयं मे

भिन्ना प्रकृतिरष्टधा ॥

bhūmir āpo 'nalo vāyuḥ
khaṃ mano buddhir eva ca
ahaṃkāra itīyaṃ me
bhinnā prakṛtir aṣṭadhā

Earth, water, fire, air,
space, mind, intellect, and
ego: These are the eight
aspects of my divided nature.

Bhagavad-Gītā, 7.4

4. अमृतस्य पुत्राः ।

amṛtasya putrāḥ

of immortality O sons

O sons of immortality.

Śvetāśvatara Upaniṣad, 2.5

1. तत्स्वयं योगसंसिद्धः कालेनात्मनि विन्दति ।

tat svayaṃ yoga-saṃsiddhaḥ kālenātmani vindati

this himself yoga-perfected with time in himself finds

He who is perfected in yoga of himself in time finds this within himself.

Bhagavad-Gītā, 4.38

2. समत्वं योग उच्यते ।

samatvaṃ yoga ucyate

balance yoga is called

Balance of mind is called yoga.

Bhagavad-Gītā, 2.48

3. अत्ता चराचरग्रहणात् ।

attā carācara-grahaṇāt

devourer movable-immovable-from taking in

Brahman is the devourer of the movable and the immovable.

Brahma Sūtra, 1.2.9

4. समानी व आकूतिः समाना हृदयानि वः ।
समानमस्तु वो मनो यथा वः सुसहासति ॥

samānī va ākūtiḥ samānā hṛdayāni vaḥ
samānamastu vo mano yathā vaḥ susahāsati

United be your purpose, harmonious be your feelings, collected be your mind, in the same way as all the various aspects of the universe exist in togetherness, wholeness.

Ṛg-Ved, 10.191.4

1. नाल्पे सुखमस्ति भूमैव सुखम् ।

nālpe sukham asti bhūmaiva sukham

not in small joy is infinite alone joy

There is no joy in smallness. Joy is in the infinite.

Chāndogya Upaniṣad, 7.23

2. अङ्गुष्ठमात्रः पुरुषो ऽन्तरात्मा सदा जनानां

हृदये सन्निविष्टः ।

aṅguṣṭha-mātraḥ puruṣo 'ntarātmā sadā janānāṃ
hṛdaye sanniviṣṭaḥ

thumb-sized puruṣa innermost Self ever of persons
in the heart residing deep inside

Deep inside the person is the puruṣa of the size of the thumb.
That is the innermost of one's Self, of one's consciousness.

Kaṭha Upaniṣad, 2.3.17

3. प्रचारः स तु विज्ञेयः ।

pracāraḥ sa tu vijñeyaḥ

The mind gets expanded in the transcendent.

Gauḍapāda's *Māṇḍūkya Kārikā*, 3.34

4. दूरेदृशं गृहपतिमथर्युम् ।

dūre-dṛśaṃ gṛha-patim atharyum

distance-seen house-owner reverberating

Far in the distance is seen the owner of the house, reverberating.

Ṛg-Ved, 7.1.1

1. शिवं शान्तमद्वैतं चतुर्थं मन्यन्ते स आत्मा स विज्ञेयः ।

śivaṃ śāntam advaitaṃ caturthaṃ manyante sa ātmā sa vijñeyaḥ

blissful peaceful undivided fourth they regard that Self that to be known

The peaceful, the blissful, the undivided is thought to be the fourth; that is the Self. That is to be known.

Nṛsiṃhottaratāpanīya Upaniṣad, 1

2. स्मृतिर्लब्धा ।

smṛtir labdhā

memory regained

I have regained memory.

Bhagavad-Gītā, 18.73

3. अथातो ब्रह्मजिज्ञासा ।

athāto brahma-jijñāsā

now from here brahman-desire to know

Now, from here, the desire to know brahman.

Brahma Sūtra, 1.1.1

4. पश्य मे योगमैश्वरम् ।

paśya me yogam aiśvaram

behold my yoga sovereign

Behold my sovereign yoga.

Bhagavad-Gītā, 9.5

1. अग्निः पूर्वेभिर्ऋषिभिरीड्यो नूतनैरुत ।

agniḥ pūrvebhir ṛṣibhir īḍyo nūtanair uta

the Ved by the ancient ṛṣis honored by the ṛṣis in the present also

The Ved was honored by the ancient ṛṣis of old in their consciousness and also by the ṛṣis in the present.

Ṛg-Ved, 1.1.2

2. अथ योगानुशासनम् ।

atha yogānuśāsanam

now yoga teaching

Now is the teaching on yoga.

Yoga Sūtras, 1.1

3. योगश्चित्तवृत्तिनिरोधः ।

yogaś citta-vṛtti-nirodhaḥ

yoga mind-fluctuation-least excited

Yoga is the least excited state of the mind. (Given earlier.)

Yoga Sūtras, 1.2

4. तदा द्रष्टुः स्वरूपे अवस्थानम् ।

tadā draṣṭuḥ svarūpe avasthānam

then of the seer in self-referral establishment

Then the seer is established in self-referral.

Yoga Sūtras, 1.3

5. वृत्तिसारूप्यमितरत्र ।

vṛtti-sārūpyam itaratra

From here, what you see you become.

Yoga Sūtras, 1.4

1. योगिनः कर्म कुर्वन्ति सङ्गं त्यक्त्वात्मशुद्धये ।

yoginaḥ karma kurvanti saṅgaṃ tyaktvātma-śuddhaye

yogis action perform attachment abandoning self-purification

Yogis, abandoning attachment, perform action for self-purification.

Bhagavad-Gītā, 5.11

2. ज्ञानविज्ञानतृप्तात्मा ।

jñāna-vijñāna-tṛptātmā

knowledge-experience-contented-Self

Knowledge and experience bring contentment.

Bhagavad-Gītā, 6.8

3. आनन्दाद्ध्येव खल्विमानि भूतानि जायन्ते ।

आनन्देन जातानि जीवन्ति ।

आनन्दं प्रयन्त्यभिसंविशन्ति ॥

ānandād dhy eva khalv imāni bhūtāni jāyante
ānandena jātāni jīvanti
ānandaṃ prayanty abhisaṃviśanti

Out of bliss these beings are born,
In bliss they are sustained,
And to bliss they go and merge again.

Taittirīya Upaniṣad, 3.6.1

1. वेदो ऽहम् ।

vedo 'ham

Veda I

I am the Veda. ***Devī Upaniṣad***, 1

2. तरति शोकमात्मवित् ।

tarati śokam ātmavit

crosses suffering Self-knower

Established in the Self, one overcomes sorrows and suffering.

Chāndogya Upaniṣad, 7.1.3

3. ब्रह्मसंस्पर्शमत्यन्तं सुखम् ।

brahma-saṃsparśam atyantaṃ sukham

brahman-contact infinite joy

Contact with brahman is infinite joy.

Bhagavad-Gītā, 6.28

4. समितिः समानी ।

samitiḥ samānī

assembly even

An assembly is significant in unity.

Ṛg-Ved, 10.191.3

5. अग्निमीळे ।

agnim īḷe

I associate myself with agni. ***Rg-Ved***, 1.1.1

1. गहना कर्मणो गतिः ।

gahanā karmaṇo gatiḥ

unfathomable of action course

Unfathomable is the course of action.

Bhagavad-Gītā, 4.17

2. स्वल्पमप्यस्य धर्मस्य त्रायते महतो भयात् ।

svalpam apy asya dharmasya trāyate mahato bhayāt

little even of this dharma delivers from great fear

Even a little of this dharma delivers from great fear.

Bhagavad-Gītā, 2.40

3. आनन्दमयो ऽभ्यासात् ।

ānandamayo 'bhyāsāt

blissful from practice

Brahman becomes blissful through practice.

Brahma Sūtra, 1.1.12

4. निमित्तमात्रं भव सव्यसाचिन् ।

nimitta-mātraṃ bhava savyasācin

instrument-only be Arjuna

Be only the instrument, Oh Arjuna.

Bhagavad-Gītā, 11.33

5. प्रत्यवायो न विद्यते ।

pratyavāyo na vidyate

obstacle not exists

No obstacle exists. *Bhagavad-Gītā*, 2.40

1. सर्वभूतस्थमात्मानं सर्वभूतानि चात्मनीक्षते ।

sarvabhūtastham ātmānaṃ sarvabhūtāni cātmanīkṣate

in all beings established Self all beings and in the Self he sees

He sees the Self in all beings, and all beings in the Self.

Bhagavad-Gītā, 6.29

2. ज्ञानाग्निदग्धकर्माणं तमाहुः पण्डितं बुधाः ।

jñānāgni-dagdha-karmāṇaṃ tam āhuḥ paṇḍitaṃ budhāḥ

knowledge-fire-burnt-action him call wise knowers of reality

Whose action is burnt up in the fire of knowledge, him the knowers of reality call wise.

Bhagavad-Gītā, 4.19

3. वश्यात्मना तु यतता शक्यो ऽवाप्तुमुपायतः ।

vaśyātmanā tu yatatā śakyo 'vāptum upāyataḥ

disciplined-man endeavoring possible to gain through proper means

Yoga can be gained through proper means by the man of endeavor who is disciplined.

Bhagavad-Gītā, 6.36

4. स तु दीर्घकालनैरंतर्यसत्कारासेवितो दृढभूमिः ।

sa tu dīrgha-kāla-nairaṃtarya-satkārāsevito dṛdha-bhūmiḥ

Yoga becomes firmly established when it has been respectfully and uninterruptedly cultivated for a long time. ***Yoga Sūtras***, 1.14

BHAGAVAD-GĪTA
CHAPTER TWO

त्रैगुण्यविषया वेदा निस्त्रैगुण्यो भवार्जुन ।
निर्द्वन्द्वो नित्यसत्त्वस्थो निर्योगक्षेम आत्मवान् ॥४५॥

traiguṇya-viṣayā vedā nistraiguṇyo bhavārjuna
nirdvandvo nitya-sattvastho niryoga-kṣema ātmavān 45

योगस्थः कुरु कर्माणि सङ्गं त्यक्त्वा धनञ्जय ।
सिद्ध्यसिद्ध्योः समो भूत्वा समत्वं योग उच्यते ॥४८॥

yogasthaḥ kuru karmāṇi saṅgaṃ tyaktvā dhanañjaya
siddhy-asiddhyoḥ samo bhūtvā samatvaṃ yoga ucyate 48

दूरेण ह्यवरं कर्म बुद्धियोगाद्धनञ्जय ।
बुद्धौ शरणमन्विच्छ कृपणाः फलहेतवः ॥४९॥

dūreṇa hy avaraṃ karma buddhi-yogād dhanañjaya
buddhau śaraṇam anviccha kṛpaṇāḥ phala-hetavaḥ 49

बुद्धियुक्तो जहातीह उभे सुकृतदुष्कृते ।
तस्माद्योगाय युज्यस्व योगः कर्मसु कौशलम् ॥५०॥

buddhi-yukto jahātīha ubhe sukṛta-duṣkṛte
tasmād yogāya yujyasva yogaḥ karmasu kauśalam 50

कर्मजं बुद्धियुक्ता हि फलं त्यक्त्वा मनीषिणः ।
जन्मबन्धविनिर्मुक्ताः पदं गच्छन्त्यनामयम् ॥५१॥

karmajaṃ buddhi-yuktā hi phalaṃ tyaktvā manīṣiṇaḥ
janma-bandha-vinirmuktāḥ padaṃ gacchanty anāmayam 51

यदा ते मोहकलिलं बुद्धिर्व्यतितरिष्यति ॥
तदा गन्तासि निर्वेदं श्रोतव्यस्य श्रुतस्य च ॥५२॥

yadā te moha-kalilaṃ buddhir vyatitariṣyati

tadā gantāsi nirvedaṃ śrotavyasya śrutasya ca 52

श्रुतिविप्रतिपन्ना ते यदा स्थास्यति निश्चला ॥
समाधावचला बुद्धिस्तदा योगमवाप्स्यसि ॥५३॥

śruti-vipratipannā te yadā sthāsyati niścalā

samādhāv acalā buddhis tadā yogam avāpsyasi 53

अर्जुन उवाच ।
स्थितप्रज्ञस्य का भाषा समाधिस्थस्य केशव ॥
स्थितधीः किं प्रभाषेत किमासीत व्रजेत किम् ॥५४॥

arjuna uvāca
sthita-prajñasya kā bhāṣā samādhi-sthasya keśava

sthita-dhīḥ kiṃ prabhāṣeta kim āsīta vrajeta kim 54

श्रीभगवानुवाच ।
प्रजहाति यदा कामान्सर्वान्पार्थ मनोगतान् ॥
आत्मन्येवात्मना तुष्टः स्थितप्रज्ञस्तदोच्यते ॥५५॥

śrī bhagavān uvāca
prajahāti yadā kāmān sarvān pārtha mano-gatān

ātmany evātmanā tuṣṭaḥ sthita-prajñas tadocyate 55

दुःखेष्वनुद्विग्नमनाः सुखेषु विगतस्पृहः ॥
वीतरागभयक्रोधः स्थितधीर्मुनिरुच्यते ॥५६॥

duḥkheṣv anudvigna-manāḥ sukheṣu vigata-spṛhaḥ

vīta-rāga-bhaya-krodhaḥ sthita-dhīr munir ucyate 56

यः सर्वत्रानभिस्नेहस्तत्तत्प्राप्य शुभाशुभम् ॥
नाभिनन्दति न द्वेष्टि तस्य प्रज्ञा प्रतिष्ठिता ॥५७॥

yaḥ sarvatrānabhisnehas tat tat prāpya śubhāśubham
nābhinandati na dveṣṭi tasya prajñā pratiṣṭhitā 57

यदा संहरते चायं कूर्मो ऽङ्गानीव सर्वशः ॥
इन्द्रियाणीन्द्रियार्थेभ्यस्तस्य प्रज्ञा प्रतिष्ठिता ॥५८॥

yadā saṃharate cāyaṃ kūrmo 'ṅgānīva sarvaśaḥ
indriyāṇīndriyārthebhyas tasya prajñā pratiṣṭhitā 58

विषया विनिवर्तन्ते निराहारस्य देहिनः ॥
रसवर्जं रसो ऽप्यस्य परं दृष्ट्वा निवर्तते ॥५९॥

viṣayā vinivartante nirāhārasya dehinaḥ
rasa-varjaṃ raso 'py asya paraṃ dṛṣṭvā nivartate 59

यततो ह्यपि कौन्तेय पुरुषस्य विपश्चितः ॥
इन्द्रियाणि प्रमाथीनि हरन्ति प्रसभं मनः ॥६०॥

yatato hy api kaunteya puruṣasya vipaścitaḥ
indriyāṇi pramāthīni haranti prasabhaṃ manaḥ 60

तानि सर्वाणि संयम्य युक्त आसीत मत्परः ॥
वशे हि यस्येन्द्रियाणि तस्य प्रज्ञा प्रतिष्ठिता ॥६१॥

tāni sarvāṇi saṃyamya yukta āsīta mat-paraḥ
vaśe hi yasyendriyāṇi tasya prajñā pratiṣṭhitā 61

ध्यायतो विषयान्पुंसः सङ्गस्तेषूपजायते ॥
सङ्गात्संजायते कामः कामात्क्रोधो ऽभिजायते ॥६२॥

dhyāyato viṣayān puṃsaḥ saṅgas teṣūpajāyate
saṅgāt saṃjāyate kāmaḥ kāmāt krodho 'bhijāyate 62

क्रोधाद्भवति संमोहः संमोहात्स्मृतिविभ्रमः ॥
स्मृतिभ्रंशाद्बुद्धिनाशो बुद्धिनाशात्प्रणश्यति ॥६३॥

krodhād bhavati saṃmohaḥ saṃmohāt smṛti-vibhramaḥ
smṛti-bhraṃśād buddhi-nāśo buddhi-nāśāt praṇaśyati 63

रागद्वेषवियुक्तैस्तु विषयानिन्द्रियैश्चरन् ॥
आत्मवश्यैर्विधेयात्मा प्रसादमधिगच्छति ॥६४॥

rāga-dveṣa-viyuktais tu viṣayān indriyaiś caran
ātma-vaśyair vidheyātmā prasādam adhigacchati 64

प्रसादे सर्वदुःखानां हानिरस्योपजायते ॥
प्रसन्नचेतसो ह्याशु बुद्धिः पर्यवतिष्ठते ॥६५॥

prasāde sarva-duḥkhānāṃ hānir asyopajāyate
prasanna-cetaso hy āśu buddhiḥ paryavatiṣṭhate 65

नास्ति बुद्धिरयुक्तस्य न चायुक्तस्य भावना ॥
न चाभावयतः शान्तिरशान्तस्य कुतः सुखम् ॥६६॥

nāsti buddhir ayuktasya na cāyuktasya bhāvanā
na cābhāvayataḥ śāntir aśāntasya kutaḥ sukham 66

इन्द्रियाणां हि चरतां यन्मनो ऽनुविधीयते ॥
तदस्य हरति प्रज्ञां वायुर्नावमिवाम्भसि ॥६७॥

indriyāṇāṃ hi caratāṃ yan mano 'nuvidhīyate

tad asya harati prajñāṃ vāyur nāvam ivāmbhasi 67

तस्माद्यस्य महाबाहो निगृहीतानि सर्वशः ॥
इन्द्रियाणीन्द्रियार्थेभ्यस्तस्य प्रज्ञा प्रतिष्ठिता ॥६८॥

tasmād yasya mahābāho nigṛhītāni sarvaśaḥ

indriyāṇīndriyārthebhyas tasya prajñā pratiṣṭhitā 68

या निशा सर्वभूतानां तस्यां जागर्ति संयमी ॥
यस्यां जाग्रति भूतानि सा निशा पश्यतो मुनेः ॥६९॥

yā niśā sarva-bhūtānāṃ tasyāṃ jāgarti saṃyamī

yasyāṃ jāgrati bhūtāni sā niśā paśyato muneḥ 69

आपूर्यमाणमचलप्रतिष्ठं समुद्रमापः प्रविशन्ति यद्वत् ॥
तद्वत्कामा यं प्रविशन्ति सर्वे स शान्तिमाप्नोति न
कामकामी ॥७०॥

āpūryamāṇam acala-pratiṣṭhaṃ samudram āpaḥ praviśanti
yadvat
tadvat kāmā yaṃ praviśanti sarve sa śāntim āpnoti na
kāma-kāmī 70

विहाय कामान्यः सर्वान्पुमांश्चरति निःस्पृहः ॥
निर्ममो निरहङ्कारः स शान्तिमधिगच्छति ॥७१॥

vihāya kāmān yaḥ sarvān pumāṃś carati niḥspṛhaḥ

nirmamo nirahaṅkāraḥ sa śāntim adhigacchati 71

एषा ब्राह्मी स्थितिः पार्थ नैनां प्राप्य विमुह्यति ॥
स्थित्वास्यामन्तकाले ऽपि ब्रह्मनिर्वाणमृच्छति ॥७२॥

eṣā brāhmī sthitiḥ pārtha naināṃ prāpya vimuhyati

sthitvāsyām anta-kāle 'pi brahma-nirvāṇam ṛcchati 72

INDEX OF GRAMMATICAL TERMS

dīrga: long vowel 2
devanāgarī: script of the "city of immortals" 4
dvandva: copulative compound; both members are principal. If compound were dissolved, members would be joined by "and." 210, 235
dvigu: "worth two cows," **karmadhāraya** compound that begins with a number 236
dvitīya: "second," second letter in each **varga** 10
dhātu: root x
nañ-samāsa: negative compound 213, 236
nāman: "name," nominal x
nipāta: indeclinable, particle x
pañcama: "fifth," fifth letter in each **varga** 10
pada-pāṭha: "word-reading," (without **sandhi**) recitation of the individual words of the Veda ix
parasmai-pada: "word for another," active endings, active voice 25, 112
puruṣa: person 5, 25
- **prathama**: "first," third 5, 25
- **madhyama**: "middle," second 5, 25
- **uttama**: "last," first 5, 25

pragṛhya: vowel not subject to **sandhi** 91, 170
prathama: "first," first letter in each **varga** 10
pradhāna: the principal member of a compound 233
prātipadika: noun stem 33
pluta: vowel held for three counts, protracted 2
bahavrīhi: compound whose principal is outside itself 236
mahā-prāṇa: aspirated 10
mātrā: count, measure, duration 2
mūrdhan: hard palate 9
mūrdhanya: retroflex 9, 22
repha: "snarl," the sound **ra** 10